an unconsidered people
the irish in london

catherine
dunne

NEW
ISLAND

AN UNCONSIDERED PEOPLE
First published 2003
by New Island
2 Brookside
Dundrum Road
Dublin 14

www.newisland.ie

The author has asserted her moral rights.

ISBN 1 902602 75 7

British Library Cataloguing in Publication Data.
A CIP catalogue record for this book is available
from the British Library.

Typeset by New Island.
Cover design by Artmark.
Photographs courtesy of the Galtymore Dance Club.
Travel Identity Card courtesy of Phyllis Izzard.
Printed in Ireland by Colour Books.

New Island received financial assistance from
The Arts Council (An Chomhairle Ealaíon), Dublin, Ireland.

10 9 8 7 6 5 4 3 2 1

*To Phyllis Izzard, for starting all of this on a
boat to Venice seventeen years ago.*

*And to James Izzard, for showing me how the original Roman
road – now the A5 – passes through Watling Street, Kilburn,
Cricklewood, Burnt Oak, Edgware and Stanmore. It then
makes its way across country through Milton Keynes,
Stratford, Oswestry and Llangollen. Finally, the same
road ends up – after 239 miles – in Holyhead,
which is where this journey begins.*

CONTENTS

Introduction

'In no other European country was emigration so
essential a prerequisite for the preservation of the society.'
– J. J. Lee, *Ireland 1912–1985: politics and society*

It is Saturday night at the Galtymore Dance Club in Cricklewood.
The mirrored globe above us revolves slowly, showering the sedate
dancers below with multicoloured shards of light. Couples, from
the barely middle-aged to the frankly elderly, waltz or quickstep to
the strains of Declan Nerney. They make smooth, stately progress
around the polished floor. There are no collisions: there's still
plenty of room. The tables at the side are filling up quickly, the bar
is doing a brisk business, but it's early yet. From beyond the not-
quite soundproof partition comes the muffled beat of Bagatelle –
for the younger people.

This is the last-remaining Irish dancehall in London. The
Round Tower, the Estate, the Garryowen, the Hammersmith
Palais, the Gresham, the Blarney – all major community centres for
the Irish in London in the 1950s and 1960s – they're all gone now.
But the Galtymore hangs on – a little frayed and faded at the edges,
to be sure, but nevertheless still *there* – a busy and buzzing focus
for the Irish still living in Kilburn and Cricklewood and beyond.

1

For the half-million Irish people who left these shores in the 1950s, places like the Galtymore were much more than somewhere to go at the weekend. They were part of a vital network of friendly faces and accents, an island of familiarity in what was, at least initially, an urban ocean of strangeness and isolation. According to Kathleen Morrissey, 'It [the Galtymore] was a great big network, really. For me, in so many ways, it was the most significant place in my life in London.'

All through the 1950s, as the stream of emigrants swelled, Irish communities throughout Britain pulled ever tighter and closer together. There was no shortage of company: four out of every five children born in Ireland between 1931 and 1941 ended up 'taking the boat', with eighty per cent of them destined for Britain.[1]

Many who took the short, uncomfortable journey on the cattle-boat hoped that the economic imperative would be a short-lived one. 'We never meant to stay,' is a constant refrain among many of the London Irish, some of them well into their fifth decade away from home. Their intention was to soon save up enough money to come back to Ireland – as indeed, some of them did. Others realised that there was nothing to come back *for*: that they were gone for good. And still others went with a sense of adventure, feeling the need to escape the mundane and impoverished reality that was Ireland in the 1950s. Mary Walker says that she went to London for 'something different', just for a year, but that 'one year's experience … somehow ended up being forty-one years of experience'. Whatever the hopes and aspirations, no two emigrant experiences were the same.

This book borrows the stories of ten people who left Ireland roughly fifty years ago. It is an attempt to feel the texture of ordinary lives in the 1950s; to celebrate extraordinary feats of survival and endurance; and to understand a little more of what happened to those who became lost, falling between the boundaries of family and state. In short, these are stories of ordinary lives, stories which take centre stage without apology. The narrators belong to that generation which it most conveniently served official Ireland to forget. Yet in their leaving, the half-million emigrants of the 1950s simultaneously prevented social revolt by providing a safety-valve for Ireland's growing economic pressures *and* laid the foundations for what would later become Ireland's 'economic miracle'.

As early as 1953, it was obvious that the attitude of official Ireland towards these emigrants was a deeply ambiguous one. On the one hand, the deepening economic crisis meant that the departure of over forty thousand people each year was a relief – those jobs, at least, did not have to be found: 'If emigration were to be stopped tomorrow, conditions favourable to social revolution might easily arise.'[2]

On the other hand, those who left were often portrayed as disloyal and self-seeking in some way. To leave de Valera's Ireland in search of a reasonable living elsewhere was somehow an obscurely selfish act. Ignoring the economic realities, de Valera neatly sidestepped pressures to help ease the plight of the emigrants in Britain by claiming:

> work is available at home, and in conditions infinitely
> better from the point of both health and morals …
> There is no doubt that many of those who emigrate
> could find employment at home at as good, or better,
> wages – and with living conditions far better – than
> they find in Britain.[3]

The stories included in this book, and the many, many more not included due to restrictions of space, give the lie to this astonishing statement. In one form or another, the reality that there was nothing at home – nothing to stay for, nothing to come back to – was expressed by everyone I met. Resignation and acceptance of that fact were always the keynotes; there is a remarkable absence of bitterness among those who succeeded in making a new life for themselves, often under difficult conditions. As Phyllis Izzard says: 'There was nothing else to do apart from take the boat.'

Thus a whole generation of Irish people did just that: they took the boat, unskilled, unprepared and unconsidered. They managed to become doubly invisible: victims of the 'diplomatic blind eye – [the] catalogue of neglect'[4] within their own country, and invisible in their host community, too, where their white skin and ability to speak English masked the urgency of their needs. Nevertheless, their legacy is, ironically, a highly visible one:

> In the 1940s and 1950s hundreds and thousands of young men and women left Ireland ... [They] contributed so much to the Irish economy when times were hard. In today's figures Irish emigrants were sending back £500–£750 million [€635–€952 million] *each year*. It is because of those remittances that we now have the Celtic Tiger economy.[5]

KILBURN AND CRICKLEWOOD: 'ANOTHER IRISH COUNTY'

The Irish in Britain had been granted immunity from immigration control since 1941. However, those travelling between Ireland and Britain in the fifties had to have their Travel Identity Card (Cárta Aitheantais Taistil) with them, so it is reasonable to assume that some official registration of the numbers arriving was ongoing. In the fifties, North London was the site of already well-established Irish communities. 'Bursting at the seams with Irish' as Mary Walker says, it was also bursting with factories and employment opportunities for newly arriving immigrants. These areas were typical examples of 'chain migration' – the phenomenon where one settled family member pulled the next one after him or her and so on until whole families made new homes in areas such as Kilburn, Cricklewood, Camden, Edgware and Brent. Cricklewood even today has the highest concentration of Irish in Britain.[6]

Working on the principle that the particular can help to illustrate the general, I decided to focus for the most part on the experiences of people who had lived and worked in these established Irish communities during the 1950s. Kilburn and Cricklewood, according to Catherine Morris (formerly of the London Irish Centre), were known as 'another Irish county'. Maybe it was because the area was close to Euston, she says – just about 'as far as you could carry a suitcase'. Huge Irish family networks developed there as a result.

However, I was also very conscious of the phenomenon of casual Irish labour, wherein the men who worked in the construction industry 'on the lump' had had to 'follow the work', moving from place to place, sometimes for years, overnighting in Salvation Army hostels or Rowton Houses for as long as a job lasted. Some of those construction industry workers, like Tony Maher, settled, often in new towns which were under construction as part of the post-war boom. They progressed from the insecurity and invisibility of 'the lump' into the tax and social insurance net – in most cases once they married and had families.

And so I went myself to Harlow, some forty miles north-east of London. Like many other 'new' towns throughout Britain at that time, Harlow provided both secure employment and housing to those prepared to work there. Joe Dunne recalls the phone call from the Council telling him to 'pick your house'. His wife, Marie, marvels at the standard of accommodation available to them: 'You could *choose* your house – a two-bedroomed or a three-bedroomed house.'

However, others were not so fortunate. Years of 'following the work' somehow became decades. Men caught in the trap of casual labour had no opportunity to participate in the settled lives of any community, Irish or otherwise. Like Willy Loman in *Death of a Salesman*, they felt 'kind of temporary', temporary about themselves in Britain, and were orientated towards that day, somewhere in the future, when they would go back to Ireland. And so they continued to live and work on the margins, accepting cash-in-hand payments, rejecting a tax and insurance system which they fundamentally mistrusted. For their entire working lives, they remained on the outskirts of comfort and security. Often cheated and lied to by those they trusted most, they led lives of increasing isolation. From having been 'doubly invisible' as young men, they now feel 'doubly marginalised' in their older years: they feel that the British state doesn't want them and, even if they could make it home, it would appear that the Irish state doesn't want them either. Despite years and years of sending home the weekly postal order – the so-called emigrant remittances – they now rightly feel that their contribution is unconsidered:

> Irish citizens returning home from Britain have no more rights than other EU nationals, a senior Irish Government official has confirmed. The Government has responded to the tide of emigrants returning to Ireland by reiterating that EU laws prevented them giving any special status. This means that Irish people returning home will have difficulties joining housing waiting lists or getting on hospital waiting lists for operations.[7]

It became very clear to me early on in this undertaking that there is no such thing as a 'typical' emigrant – or immigrant. Writing of the Jewish experience of involuntary migration, Michael Prior suggests that there are, in fact, no typical Diaspora conditions: 'they exhibit a wide spectrum, from total assimilation to new total isolation,' reflecting the different social level of each individual as well as their personal preferences.[8]

It also became clear that the most significant difficulty inherent in this project was going to be what to leave out, rather than what to include. As it was, this series of interviews developed more or less organically – rather like chain migration itself. Phyllis Izzard insisted I record Kathleen Morrissey's story, who then insisted I listen to Sheila Dillon, who insisted I met with Fr Seamus Fullam, and so on. And for my part, I had no agenda, other than acting as midwife to the many stories I was told openly, honestly and often with a great deal of humour despite obvious hardships.

I am aware that these ten interviews reflect what are commonly regarded as the 'success stories'. For every happy ending, or at least a contented and accepting one, there is a myriad of other stories – of isolation, deprivation, prejudice. However, I took the decision very early on to explore the plight of the marginalised Irish through the experienced eyes of those already working in the field – to do so at second remove, as it were. The London Irish Centre at Camden and the Emigrant Liaison Committee in Co. Mayo were both extremely helpful in this regard. Besides, it seemed wrong to seek out people who had already suffered enough: one of the phenomena of ageing is the increasing acuteness of long-term memory. Asking people to recall the trajectory of their lives several decades later – people who, by their own definition, had led lives of failure – was, I felt, no business of mine.

'SNAGGING TURNIPS FOR THREE HA'PENCE A DRILL'[9]

Driving through the countryside in post-Celtic-Tiger Ireland, it's clear that the past is indeed 'another country'. What makes it even more unfamiliar is that in this case the past is not that distant at all – a mere fifty years or so. Tidy towns and villages, hanging baskets, arts centres are all very far removed from the rural Ireland that still lives on in the memories of those who were forced to leave it. For Tony Maher, the impetus to leave Kildare was supplied by the realisation that 'snagging turnips for three ha'pence a drill didn't appeal to me'.

For Stephen Croghan, who worked in London on and off during the fifties and sixties, a sense of place and home are tangible. His story is a central one in that it illustrates starkly what drove people to Britain in the first place: that is, it focuses on what people left behind – rather than what faced them in London on their arrival. The picture he paints of rural Ireland in the forties and fifties is as vivid as it is distressing. Despite the pious aspirations of de Valera, who longed for a country populated by those 'who valued material wealth only as the basis for right living

… who were satisfied with frugal comfort' and who lived in a country 'bright with cosy homesteads … [with] the romping of sturdy children … the contests of athletic youths and the laughter of comely maidens',[10] the reality was very different.

Stephen remembers the exodus from Roscommon to Britain that started in the forties: 'It was that or starvation.' He recalls the typical working week for those on the land: 'six o'clock in the morning until six o'clock in the evening … living in an outhouse. That's the way it was.'

And so men queued for the train to take them to the boat and on to the construction jobs which were so plentiful all over Britain. They waited at the station, with a tag on their coat 'same as you'd tie a parcel'. On each tag was the man's destination and the name of the builder employing him. According to Stephen, 'hundreds went out … like that, hundreds'. It's a memory also shared by Kevin Casey from Ennis. As well as the queues at the station, he remembers the agent who got a commission for each man he delivered to McAlpine. Kevin says 'There was a lot of misery left behind in those days. Perhaps we're not as angry as we could be because we did well ourselves.'

Anne O'Neill's recollections of rural Roscommon are similarly bleak, in contrast to the 'cosy homesteads' and 'frugal comfort' envisaged by de Valera: 'We had no electric, no toilet, nothing like that … We had to bring the water in from outside. The toilet was wherever you could find a space.'

She remembers her elderly grandmother, when the day's work was done. 'She'd just sit by the fire, looking into it, rocking her head up and down, up and down.'

It is no wonder that people fled the Irish countryside in droves; the wonder is that there was anybody left behind.

'CULTURE SHOCK'

Fr Seamus Fullam has worked among the Irish in London for close on five decades now. He identifies 'culture shock' as the main difficulty facing young Irish immigrants on their arrival in Britain. 'Everything was so completely different,' he says. The sense of isolation was acute, the longing for community intense. Young men, in particular, seemed to suffer from extreme loneliness. It seems that young women had a better network of family, church and friends to which they clung on arrival – or perhaps they simply accessed that network more readily. The London Irish Centre in Camden played a pivotal role in this regard in the 1950s. It provided a welcome for the newly arrived and offered a wealth of information on accommodation, work opportunities, churches and social clubs. Many new arrivals landed, like Joe Dunne, with just a fiver in their pocket. They needed to find work at once – there was no hand outstretched to help, and the landlady needed her money. It was quite a shock to the system; among all those who spoke to me of their initial experiences, there was general agreement that 'you had to grow up very quickly'.

It's worth remembering that the Irish *did* qualify for Social Welfare payments in 1950s Britain – and had done so since an agreement was signed between the two governments in 1921. But, according to Fr Jerry Kivlehan of the London Irish Centre in Camden, many Irish were refused their Social Welfare entitlements due to 'ignorance on the part of British civil servants'. It was not uncommon for those working in the Social Welfare system in the UK to be unaware of the 1921 agreement and they treated Irish workers with hostility. Often, people were unable to fight for what was due to them and, like Stephen Croghan, believed that the Irish were entitled to nothing, unlike those from the Commonwealth, for example, who were deemed to have a natural right to live and work in the 'mother country'.

Inevitably, with what seems to have been an official attitude of intolerance towards the huge numbers of Irish men and women arriving every year, many of the most vulnerable were to slip through the net of the Social Security system and, to all intents and purposes, they simply disappeared, some never contacting their families again.

'THE PUB BECAME A COMMUNITY OF SORTS'

On various occasions over the past three years, everyone I spoke to – both those who frequented pubs themselves and took a drink, and those who still had their Pioneer pin – agreed that huge numbers of young Irish men developed alcohol-related problems *after* their arrival in Britain. Alcoholism developed in many cases as a response to the sense of loneliness and isolation that many experienced. Drinking temporarily deadened the pain of grief and loss. Thus alcohol became valued as an anaesthetic, rather than as part of social interaction.

Kevin Casey, who managed a five-bar business in London, says that many of the Irish, particularly those involved in casual labour, had nowhere else to go but to the pub: 'These men used to stay in digs, but digs didn't want you there in the evenings … That's why the pub became a ghetto system … a community of sorts.'

But there was an altogether more sinister reason for long, alcohol-filled nights in the pub. Those who worked in the construction industry were often paid weekly by cheque. Deeply mistrustful of banks and official agencies of any sort, they were forced to cash their cheques in the pub. According to Catherine Morris, 'although the cheque would be handed in to be cashed at six, the money was not handed over until midnight. You had to drink all night to get your money.'

To add insult to injury, many of the firms which carried out this practice were Irish. Fr Fullam makes the point that there were indeed Irish firms 'that got rich on the back of exploiting their own'. Catherine Morris agrees. She says that there are many elderly Irish construction workers who are angry and bitter at the level of exploitation they endured. Now suffering from the health problems that inevitably follow years of harsh and unsafe working conditions, they find themselves with no financial cushion.

'The Irish companies did it to their own,' she explains. 'These men worked all their lives in the belief that they were paying their stamps. The money was deducted from their wages, but no contributions were ever paid on their behalf.'

Such companies are among those now being fêted as Irish 'success stories.'

Anecdotes abound about the Irish being the 'hardest on their own people', as Kevin Casey puts it. Long queues would form every morning at London Road in Elephant and Castle, Camden Tube station and the Crown pub on Cricklewood Broadway. The Irish ganger-men had the power to decide who got work that day and who didn't. Those men depending on each day's casual labour were, literally, at their foremen's mercy:

> Sometimes, a man would be taken out on a job, and
> the ganger-men took a dislike to him. They'd just
> dump him in the street and tell him to 'find your own
> so-and-so way home'... If you didn't buy your drink,
> you wouldn't be picked up the following day either.

Fr Fullam, recounting the experience of his parishioners over the years, agrees. He says that 'the Irish ... made the worst foremen. Some of them ... were tyrants. Many of the men I met through the Catholic club told me they were delighted when they got an Englishman as their foreman.'

'No cats, no dogs, no children, no Irish, no blacks'[11]

Signs such as this, advertising accommodation, were common in shop windows all over 1950s London. I think it's reasonable to speculate that there is a close relationship between one's standard of employment and the quality of housing one enjoys. That being the case, the accommodation on offer to casual labourers was often very poor indeed.

The picture of 'one room in Cricklewood or Kilburn',

sometimes shared by several men with 'mattresses on the floor', is a recurring one. As the Irish moved up in the world, they often became landlords themselves, owning large houses which they then rented out to their countrymen. Fellow-feeling was not part of the transaction. According to Anne O'Neill, 'the Irish exploited their own' by offering appalling living conditions to those who had no choice but to endure them. Men working 'on the lump' with no security, often subsisting on a day-to-day basis, could not afford the luxury of choice.

And of course, there were those who could access no form of housing at all, for various complex and interrelated reasons. Homelessness often accompanied alcoholism and/or mental-health related problems. According to Catherine Morris, those men and women who had mental health problems co-existing with alcohol-related problems found themselves in a catch-22 situation. They couldn't access social services unless they detoxed first, and they couldn't detox 'because they didn't have the mental resources to do so'.

Research reveals that problems of inadequate housing and homelessness are associated

> with a disproportionate number of Irish people in
> Britain today ... The Irish also represent a quarter of
> homeless day centre users ... [yet the Irish represent]
> only 3.8% of the population of Greater London ... A
> report by CARA found that many local authorities
> and Housing Associations do not keep the necessary
> data to monitor Irish applicants. In fact, only 8 out of
> 60 Housing Associations provide accurate analysis of
> Irish applications.[12]

It would appear that even in this most basic of human requirements – the need for shelter – the difficulties of the marginalised Irish are once again invisible or, simply, unconsidered. Figures show that as many as two in three, or sixty per cent, of London's homeless are Irish,[13] and that 'Irish born people are more strongly clustered in social class V, the lowest grouping, than any other major ethnic group in Britain.'[14]

On the other hand, Fr Fullam remarks gratefully that there are countless cases where English landladies 'mothered' the young men who came to them for lodgings, treating them very kindly and looking after them as they would look after their own. This was the experience of Tony Maher and Joe Dunne, both of whom remember their own landladies with great fondness.

Anne O'Neill agrees that she was one of the fortunate ones, able to move eventually from rented rooms to owning her own home. She tells of some of the pettier restrictions often imposed on tenants. She and her husband Harry once lived in the home of an Irish landlady in Cricklewood:

> We had to make an appointment to have a bath. We
> had to be in by a certain time at night, too, even though
> we were married. Doors were locked at eleven o'clock
> … It was often difficult to find accommodation.

Kathleen Morrissey remembers one occasion when she had to keep her mouth firmly closed so as not to reveal her identity. She and her husband, Philip, went for an interview for a flat. But her accent, she says, was much too Irish. 'We had to manage that very carefully,' she says. And indeed, success at getting that flat in Wendover Court in Enfield, North London, was balanced on a knife-edge. By pure coincidence, an Irish neighbour was working on the road just outside where the couple's interview was to take place. Kathleen was terrified. If anyone had seen the friendly exchange between them, 'that', she says, 'would have been that'.

There were those for whom the house came with the job, an incalculable benefit for people such as Joe Dunne, Kevin Casey and Tony Maher in Harlow. Anne O'Neill and her husband Harry, living in West Hendon (between Cricklewood and Edgware), needed considerable input from family to keep a decent roof over their heads. Anne has always worked full time, 'even with five children', and it was with the assistance of her mother and sister-in-law that she and Harry kept all the domestic wheels turning. This, she says, was common practice.

It was also common to find yourself without a home once the first baby was born. 'Lots of places wouldn't accept children,' Sheila Dillon remembers. One solution was to send the baby back to relatives in Ireland until the couple could afford to get a place of their own. This was what Máire Graham, Sheila's lifelong friend, was forced to do. The effects of that separation on parents and children must have been deeply painful: yet another sense of dislocation and loss for those trying to forge a living in circumstances not of their own choosing.

Mary Walker remembers her 'palace in Kilburn' – to this day, she still has 'nightmares about that room': sparse, grey, backing onto the railway, with a gas ring that pulled out of the wall. She remembers it all without self-pity: 'That's the way it was.' After she married, a good job in the building society enabled her and her husband eventually to own their own house in Edgware, where she lived for over thirty years.

Phyllis Izzard went as a young bride to Huntington and endured thirteen years there. It was then 'a brand new town, just in the process of being built'. The house came with her husband Larry's new job. She hated every minute of her time there. There were virtually no Irish living in Huntington at the time, to be Catholic was to be the outsider and she remembers asking her husband if 'he'd taken me there to bury me'.

'The Catholic social clubs were a tremendous asset'[15]

Once work and accommodation are secured, social interaction is, for most people, pretty high on their agenda. In the young Irish immigrants' early years in London, social life tended to revolve around dancing for women and the pub for men. Most Catholic parish churches, too, had a social club attached to them in the

1950s. Fr Seamus Fullam believes that these clubs had a most important social and religious role: 'After work and ... at weekends, the men could come and play cards or darts and socialise with other people ... The clubs also kept them in contact with the Church and their duties.'

Men and women met future spouses there, and in later years they brought their children to events hosted by their local club. In that way, the clubs also became a meeting-point for second-generation Irish, a further reinforcement of community and belonging. Kevin Casey agrees that 'they were marvellous places, great social centres ... If anybody was sick, or needed a couple of hundred pounds to go back to Ireland or to bury somebody, it was there.'

However, Joe and Marie Dunne feel that the clubs encouraged the culture of drinking among lonely people and don't understand why every centre 'had to have a bar'. For Mary Walker, working among friendly faces in the Edgware social club was a new lease of life after her marriage broke up and helped her, she says, to rediscover 'my sense of humour'.

While the Catholic social clubs were thriving in the fifties and sixties, their role has diminished significantly in recent years and many of them have now closed. The needs of second-generation Irish are different. In some cases, their closure created bad feeling.

According to Kevin Casey, 'those clubs cleared the debts of many a church'. However, once that debt was paid, the clubs were closed without ceremony. 'Off you go now lads, the debt is paid, and we don't want to be known as a drinking club any longer.'

This sense of abandonment was even stronger among some of the more marginalised Irish, bewildered at the lack of practical help available to them in Britain. Their needs were much more fundamental than having access to a social club. Many of them could not understand why the Catholic Church in their adopted country did not play a more dominant social role. Kevin Casey recalls men asking him: 'Why won't the Catholic Church over here build hostels for us?'

F. H. Boland, then Ireland's Ambassador to the Court of St James, notified de Valera's government as early as July 1951 of the appalling conditions in which vast numbers of Irish emigrants were living. He cites in particular the clergy's interest 'in keeping the Irish together in individual houses, as opposed to taking digs in English households'.[16] It seems that the Church's fear was that the atmosphere in English households might not be conducive to the men's continuing practice of their Catholic faith. Such emphasis on spiritual welfare had led to some truly horrific situations, such as one in Southwark, South London, which Boland cites, 'where the local canon approved of having 150 Irishmen living in "three smallish houses" because "the men were kept together in accommodation run by a man of good character".'[17]

However, on an individual, if not an institutional level, it is clear that many Catholic priests did everything they could to alleviate the sufferings of their parishioners. Names such as Fr Eamon Casey, Fr Tom Kiernan of Quex Road, Fr Dore of the same church and Fr Fullam are names that keep being mentioned, the most high-profile of those being Eamon Casey, whose sterling work in the 1960s in housing the Irish is still remembered and much appreciated.

Many people agreed that their religion continued to play an important part in their lives after they left home. Most continued to practise their faith in Britain, albeit in a different form. There was more freedom to practise contraception, for example, or, indeed, to escape from a bad marriage if necessary, whereas the Irish Catholic culture would have kept you firmly in your place. Phyllis Izzard reflects on the sense of control she had over her life at a very difficult time: 'I mightn't have left the marriage if I'd been living at home in Ireland … We were several years ahead of life at home … in that respect.'

What emerged from most of the exchanges I had with Irish women living in London was that life away from Ireland offered the kind of freedom and scope for personal development that simply would not have been possible for them had they stayed at home. Irish patterns of emigration differ from our European counterparts – for the latter, the typical emigrant was male, usually bringing wife and children with him. Not so in the case of Ireland. In her introduction to *Irish Women in England*, Clare Barrington writes that:

> Irish emigration is a remarkable story of female self-determination. During most decades since the 1880s, more women than men have emigrated from Ireland. The vast majority of these women were single, younger than their male counterparts, and travelled alone. This large, sustained emigration of single females is an anomaly in the history of European emigration, as women from other countries did, generally, emigrate with husbands and fathers.[18]

'THOSE POOR GIRLS WERE TERRIFIED AT THEIR PREDICAMENT'[19]

Another area in which the Catholic Church, the Legion of Mary and the Crusade of Rescue were active was in the care of young Irish girls who became pregnant outside marriage. 'The shame was so great', says Fr Fullam, 'that they had to leave the country.' He is very critical of the culture in Ireland which was obsessed with sexual sin to the extent that all that negativity was projected onto the 'poor girls' who became the victims of such an 'unchristian' way of looking at the world. In this context, to 'take the boat' in the fifties has a significantly different undertone from 'taking the boat' today, but each journey points to a similar abandonment of women in trouble. Shame them, ignore them or export them. Or better again, all three. Anything as long as they go away.

Hundreds of girls arrived at Euston and other points in the

1950s, newly pregnant and very afraid. For Sheila Dillon, looking after them became her 'mission', and she dedicated years of her life to providing shelter for them, minding them and their babies and arranging adoptions. She, too, is highly critical of the culture in Ireland that allowed Magdalen-laundry-type institutions, such as that at Kanturk in Castlepollard. Here, girls were virtually enslaved and offered no escape unless their babies were adopted. Sheila Dillon is still indignant, over forty years later, at the treatment meted out to those young women at the hands of the nuns. There were some nuns there, she says, eyes glinting, 'and the softest part of them was their false teeth'.

If you couldn't arrive home in 1950s Ireland with a child born out of wedlock, you certainly couldn't come home with a black child born out of wedlock. Yet, according to Anne O'Neill, there were many such children born to Irish mothers and Afro-Caribbean fathers in London. London Transport Welfare, for example, looked after many such children while their parents worked and paid a proportion of their wages for their upkeep. She says:

> They were beautiful children … but [those women] couldn't bring them home. [They] would go home to Ireland for Christmas as usual, leaving their children behind. Mind you, that didn't just happen with mixed-race children – many young women had babies here that their families back in Ireland knew nothing about.

And sometimes the grandparents in Ireland went on not knowing for the rest of their lives. Meanwhile, all those young mothers, who had no option during those years but to give their babies away, have had to live ever since with the double burdens of grief and secrecy.

And that can be no easy load to carry.

'WHY DON'T THEY JUST PULL THE PLUG AND LET IT GO DOWN?'[20]
One issue which formed a lively part of all the discussions I've had with the London Irish is their response to the Troubles in

Northern Ireland. Every individual was very clear, and very anxious that I understood, that to be Irish was no hindrance whatever in the workplace when it came to promotion. There was general agreement that the 'English are a most tolerant people'. Tony Maher, Kevin Casey, Anne O'Neill and Joe Dunne all stress quite specifically that their 'Irishness' never went against them in their jobs.

However, when it came to the conflict in the North, everybody felt, at one stage or another, 'uncomfortable to be Irish'. Mary Walker remembers the 'sly remarks', that she was supposed to overhear, about what a terrible place Ireland had to be. Phyllis Izzard makes the distinction between not feeling 'ashamed to be Irish' and not wanting to 'shout it from the rooftops'. Public anger in Britain was intense when the IRA campaign 'on the mainland' was at its height. The bombs at Harrods, Staples Corner, Hendon, and the never-ending bomb-scares in central London, all contributed to a situation where to be Irish meant to keep your head down, not to draw attention to yourself. Joe Dunne was unable to work with his usual contractor in the underground armaments store, simply because he was Irish. No Irishmen, no men with prison records allowed. His response was simply to say: 'It was understandable, wasn't it?'

Tony Maher took the decision to tackle the 'wall of embarrassment' around the subject of the North, rather than pretend it wasn't happening. He says it was difficult to know who was the more embarrassed – the Irish or the English. All of the interviewees, at one stage or another, professed amazement at how ignorant English people tended to be about Ireland. Apart from the 'pigs in the kitchen' stereotype, they learned that the British public, for the most part, had no awareness that the North of Ireland was ruled by Westminster. Nor had they even the remotest idea of what fuelled the ongoing conflict.

But, says Tony Maher, 'Why should they? At home [in Kildare

on holiday] … I'd be told to "Shut up about the North. We don't want to know." So how can you blame the English for not knowing?'

Stephen Croghan, Tony Maher and Joe Dunne all express themselves quite forcefully on the point of 'reverse prejudice'. In other words, they say they are tired and fed-up of Irish people 'giving out about England'. They got 'a good living there', they say, and have no time for those who stir up trouble about their host country. 'England has been good to us.'

And they, I venture to suggest, have been good to England.

We discussed many other issues in the back and forth that accompanied these interviews: for example, the nature of identity for second-generation Irish, the experiences of the returning emigrant, the changes in Irish society. All of these, I feel, belong to the 'post-emigration' experience and are best explored in the concluding chapter once the following stories have been both savoured and absorbed.

It is difficult to find the words to thank all of the following people who welcomed me into their homes and into their confidence with warmth, candour and no small measure of emotion: Phyllis Izzard, Kevin Casey, Kathleen Morrissey, Mary Walker, Stephen Croghan, Fr Seamus Fullam, Sheila Dillon, Tony Maher, Anne O'Neill and Joe and Marie Dunne.

Catherine Dunne
May 2003

NOTES

Chapter title: see Kevin Casey's interview

[1] Tim Pat Coogan, *Wherever Green is Worn*, Hutchinson, London, 2000, p. xiii

[2] *Leader*, Christmas 1953, as quoted by J. J. Lee, *Ireland 1912–1985: politics and society*, CUP, Cork, 1989, p. 374

[3] Tim Pat Coogan, *De Valera: long fellow, long shadow*, Hutchinson, London, 1993, p. 663

[4] Tim Pat Coogan, *Wherever Green is Worn*, Hutchinson, London, 2000, p. xiii

[5] *Mayo News*, 2001. Author's italics.

[6] Michael J. Curran, *Across the Water: the acculturation and health of Irish people in London*, Edmund Rice Resource Centre, 2003

[7] *Irish Post*, April 1999

[8] Michael Prior, *Zionism and the State of Israel: a moral inquiry*, Routledge, London, 1999

[9] See Tony Maher's interview

[10] Eamon de Valera, St Patrick's Day address, 1943, *Speeches and Statements by Eamon de Valera: 1917–73*, Gill and Macmillan, Dublin, and St Martin's Press, New York, 1990

[11] See Anne O'Neill's interview

[12] Catherine Mary Morris, 'Why do Irish construction workers remain at the margins of the Social Security System?', MA in Public and Social Administration, Brunel University, 2001

[13] *Mirror*, November 21st 2000

[14] Fr Paul Byrne, OMI, *Reality Magazine*, October 1998

[15] See Fr Seamus Fullam's interview

[16] Tim Pat Coogan, *De Valera: long fellow, long shadow*, Hutchinson, London, 1993, p. 664

[17] Ibid.

[18] Clare Barrington, *Irish Women in England*, Cork University Press, 1997

[19] See Fr Fullam's interview

[20] See Mary Walker's interview

B 78163

Serial No.

CÁRTA AITHEANTAIS TAISTIL.

TRAVEL IDENTITY CARD.

Le h-Aghaidh Taistil idir Éire agus
Bhreatáin Mhór amháin.

*For Travel between Ireland and Great
Britain only.*

Baill ar feadh cúig bliana ó dáta eisiúna.

Valid for five years from date of issue.

R.B. Ross.
Wt.12,10,13,14, 1
PP.   also in respect
                      of daughter
                      P. LANNON

Em Barnon

4 AUG 1950

Síniú an tSealbhóra ⎱ *Anastasia Lannon*
Signature of Holder ⎰

Dáta Eisiúna ⎱ 9 · 7 · 50
Date of Issue ⎰

B 78163

Serial Number

Sloinne ⎱ LANNON
Surname ⎰

Ainmneacha ⎱ ANASTATIA
Christian Name ⎰

Sloinne a hAthar ⎱ COMMY
Maiden Name ⎰

Seoladh ⎱ GRANGE MOONCOIN
Address ⎰   CO KILKENNY

Gairm ⎱ HOUSE WIFE
Profession ⎰

Dáta Breithe ⎱ 30 · 12 · 1901
Date of Birth ⎰

Áit Bhreithe ⎱ MOONCOIN
Place of Birth ⎰

'THERE WAS NOTHING ELSE TO DO
APART FROM TAKE THE BOAT'

Phyllis Izzard is a highly intelligent, articulate woman in her sixtieth year. She is open and humorous and gives the impression of great competence allied to warmth and joie de vivre.

Can you tell me something about your original decision to leave Ireland and come to London?

The first and the most important reason was the death of my father. My mother had died a few years previously. I'd been sent away to boarding-school when I was eleven because her health was so poor.

Sadly, my father died of a burst appendix and peritonitis six years later, and there I was, on my own at home. All my family were already here in London. It was the obvious choice at the end of the day: for me to come and live with my family.

Why had your brothers and sisters come away at that time?

Everyone was long gone before me. I was the youngest of all of them – the brother nearest in age to me was then twenty-six. They'd all left a long time before my father died because there was no work for them at home. Simply no work. There was nothing else to do, really, apart from take the boat.

What are your memories of Mooncoin from those days?

My memories of Mooncoin from that time are not at all vivid. Any memories I have would be mostly from before I was eleven, and they tend to be a bit faded. I do remember my Nana well. She was a lovely old lady who wore a shawl and gave me a beautiful china cup and saucer for my fifth birthday – a treasured possession. I also remember going to visit my Aunt Mary with Mammy on Sunday afternoons for tea. Aunt Mary always looked really nice, and she had a little shop at the front of the house. At eleven I went away to boarding-school and lost touch with Mooncoin a bit. I do remember in my teens having long summer holidays from school and really looking forward to getting home.

I had a special friend called Mary who lived close by. We used to get up to all the usual teenage things, including having a huge interest in boys. In fact we came very close to falling out over a boy. We all used to meet down at the river on an evening and one of the boys liked me – his name was Christy. During a bit of horseplay one evening he kissed me. Mary was not amused. Unfortunately, my father was extremely strict so any sort of romance was out of the question. Mind you, we did manage to see each other from time to time and also to smuggle a few letters in and out of boarding-school. All very innocent stuff but something I have never forgotten.

Mooncoin is a little village, seven miles from Waterford. If you blinked, you'd pass through it and wouldn't know. In those days it was a small village and, in a lot of respects, a poor village. And my parents were no different from anyone else.

Where did people from Mooncoin go for work?

A lot of the lads would have worked for the bigger farmers. One of my brothers worked for the Council for a while, one worked in the tannery in Portlaw and thereafter I suppose people would go to Waterford. There was an iron foundry in Waterford and in later years there was a paper mill – places like that. I was too young to have any really accurate memories, but I know that work in those days was scarce – even more scarce than in the years when I came to leave.

So there was no way that my mother and father were able to look after a family like ours, once everybody got bigger. I was the youngest of ten children – seven that survived. They all had to go off and make their own way.

Tell me about some of the things your Dad did in order to feed the family.

My father was great, God bless him. He had been in the British Army during the 1914–18 War, and, as a result of that, he had a pension. The pension was very handy, of course, but he still had to do a whole lot of other things to scratch a living. He always managed to feed us because he was a great man for growing things – we never went short in that respect.

My father would do anything to raise a shilling. He'd do a bit of thatching, for example – in fact he was a very good thatcher. They used to call him Jack-Two-Loads because he always brought double what he needed. The other men'd tease him when they went down to the river to cut the reeds. 'How many loads will we need, Jack?' they'd ask him. 'You'd better bring two, just in case' – he'd give the same answer every time.

He used to mend shoes for people, too, even boots that seemed to be well beyond repair. My mother used to say 'How in the name of God are you going to do anything with them?' But he would – he'd remake them, virtually. He'd fish as well. Whenever he could get two boats and four crew together, he'd do a bit of salmon fishing using the nets. The fishmongers from Waterford would send a lorry out to the villages, and, if you'd fish to sell, you'd put a post outside with a bit of white rag tied to it and the fish lorry would stop. It was not at all unusual to see several salmon on the floor of our kitchen after my father'd been out for a night's fishing. Most would be sold, but some would be kept for the home as well.

We used to keep chickens, too, and the boys would go after the rabbits. My mother would insist that we each knew how to gut a fish and pluck a chicken. That's why this girl has a weak stomach to this day. *And* it's why I never eat fish or chicken: too much blood and guts. We were very well fed.

We used to have a lot of fruit because we had a sizeable orchard – apple trees and plums and gooseberries, pears and blackcurrants and the divil knows what. Now, whoever was earliest at the market in Waterford would get the best price for their fruit. The story goes that, this morning, my father must have overslept or something, and he went off late to Waterford and didn't get too good a price for his fruit. So he decided to cut his losses and buy himself a couple of barrels of herring to sell around the villages on his way home.

In the meantime, my mother had gone to the village, and there's my father selling herrings door to door. The poor woman came home mortified, absolutely mortified. 'Oh, your father's below in the village selling herrings. I'll never show my face again!' And she only going for her messages, God rest her soul.

Anyway, as usual, Jack-Two-Loads had far too many herrings and he decided to sell them all around the outlying villages. By this time, it was very late at night. On his way home, he met a fellow that he knew. They were sort of friends – more a love-hate relationship, really, I suppose – and your man had a field of cabbage ready for cutting.

So, in the moonlight, my father relieved him of his crop and went straight back into Waterford and sold the cabbages. So he didn't do too bad out of his initial load of fruit! He got his good price in the end.

Well, it was live by fair means or foul.

You were the last child left at home?

Yes, I was the last of ten – seven of us living. My poor mother, God rest her soul, lost three. One very early on – it might even have been the first, but I'm not sure. There were so many of us I tend to forget.

My sister, Anastasia, remembers my mother being in a hell of a state when she lost one of the babies: absolutely freaking out, beating the pillows and all the rest of it. She'd found her dead in her bed. And there was another child seven years after me – his name was Joseph – by which time Mammy would have been forty-seven. It was far too late for my mother to be having children. He died as an infant, too.

From there on in, my mother's health went downhill, and I was sent away to school. My father was particularly keen that I get an education. He had a great sense of responsibility and he was a forward-thinking man. He could see what lay ahead, and he knew that they weren't going to be around forever to look after me. As it turned out Mammy died when I was thirteen, three weeks before I made my confirmation. Going away to school was an expensive business but Daddy, being a resourceful man as usual, sold a small piece of land that we had, which was away from the home place. He sold it to an Englishman who used to come on holiday and had some romantic idea about building a house there. Daddy just forgot to tell him it had no right of way never mind building permission. Well, it paid for a trip to Clery's to buy my new uniform for school.

It was the right decision, to send me away to school, but I put in some very lonely times. I remember looking out the window of the school library in Carrick-on-Suir and being able to see across the bridge: I could go home that way, across the bridge, and into Portlaw, then back across the river and home. I remember sitting there, not knowing which was worse: the ache in my heart to go home, or the ache in my feet after the long walks with the nuns on

Sundays – bloody treks, they were. It took a long time to get used to the routine of boarding-school.

You must have been very lonely after your Dad died.

Oh, I was. I'd already been lonely in boarding-school, but I felt I'd be twice as lonely now with Daddy gone. He used to visit me every week during term-time.

I'm sure I could have stayed on at school, that my family in London would have supported me financially. But I couldn't bear the thought of being the only one left at home. I don't think I'd have been able for that sort of loneliness. I really felt that I had no choice but to leave. That's one of the biggest regrets I have about going to England. I really didn't have a choice.

My father died on Christmas Eve. We'd planned to travel to London for Christmas, but the weather that year was so ferocious that we abandoned the idea. The journey in those days was quite something – a whole day and a night, virtually, travelling.

He called me early on Christmas Eve, in agony, God love him. I had to go to the village to get help. I remember there was snow on the ground. I trudged off to Mooncoin, where they phoned for the doctor. By the time the doctor came, my father was seriously ill. The doctor said he'd call for the priest and the ambulance. He told me quite bluntly: 'Your father's dying.'

My father really didn't want to go to hospital. I think he realised he was dying, and he kept begging me 'Don't send me to hospital – please don't send me to hospital. Let me stay at home.'

Of course, they took him. But because we technically lived in Kilkenny, they took him to Kilkenny hospital, which is thirty-six miles away over rough roads, rather than to Waterford, which is a lot nearer. So what chance did the man stand? I got into the ambulance to kiss him goodbye and he told me 'Look after yourself. Be a good girl.'

When we came back from Mass on Christmas morning, the

telegram was there to say he had died. A neighbour contacted one of my sisters in London and I was able to talk to her on the phone. With her instructions and a lot of courage, I got myself ready to organise the funeral.

I cycled into Waterford with my friend Mary on the following day, chose the coffin and the robe and everything. The family came home from London, and we buried my father in Mooncoin.

Within a couple of weeks, we'd made the decision that I was leaving school. And by the end of January, I was in London.

I was seventeen.

What were your first impressions when you arrived in London?

I had been to London numerous times before, so I wasn't a complete stranger to the appearance of the place, which is so completely different aesthetically to Ireland. I remember being there as a child of seven or eight and arriving at Paddington station and looking at the clock and thinking: 'I have never in my life seen a clock so big!' So in that way it wasn't so bad, but there were other bits which were absolutely awful.

It takes a long while – or it took me a long while – to get used to the fact that people didn't speak to you in the street. I couldn't understand what was the matter with all these miserable divils who wouldn't bid you the time of day. I'd also just come out of boarding-school, which is a very sheltered life. To be suddenly mixing with girls of my own age who'd had a different upbringing, who were well up there with what was going on, with the pop charts and all the latest dances and so on – it was a bit of a shock. Not that we were totally behind the times in that respect, but there was a limited amount of music that you were allowed in boarding-school, and you certainly weren't allowed rock 'n' roll.

I felt isolated at times when I came here first, because I wasn't part of the set. I had a lot of catching up to do.

What was your first job when you came to London?

That was an interesting one as well: how I earned my living then is how I've always earned my living, ever since I came to this country, but it was not my chosen path. I somehow got railroaded into accountancy and I still continue to work in that field. At that time, had I not had to leave home, my choice would have been to go to teacher training college. Either that, or I would have joined the Civil Service. A lot of girls from the country did that: they went off to Dublin to the Civil Service. It was a great escape for some of them, to get off to Dublin and have a good old time.

And I wonder how my chosen path would have turned out. I had this strange idea that I couldn't possibly go to school in London, that education here would be completely different from education at home, so I decided I had to go to work. I lived with my eldest sister in Barnet. She and her husband didn't have any children, so I was like her offspring.

I was very cushioned in that I came to live with family, in nice surroundings, in Barnet. I wasn't coming here to live in a room, lonely, and maybe in an inner-city area. In that respect, I had it easy, I suppose, in comparison to a lot of people.

Anyway, I thought that one of the things I might like to do was hairdressing, and my sister went ballistic. 'You're not wasting your education to go flippin' hairdressing!' She had decided that I was going into an office, whether I liked it or not. After a chat with a Youth Employment officer, I was sent to a company in New Barnet called Maws. They may still exist today, and they did all sorts of things like babies' bottles, teats, baby creams and so on. I got a job there, in the filing office.

There was one whole department devoted to filing. Can you imagine how different that was from the way things are now? One whole group of people that did nothing except filing and post? That's where I started my illustrious career. I wasn't at all bored, because it was a totally new experience for me. One of the things I found difficult was that I was dealing with English people who spoke differently – I didn't always understand what they were saying. I worried a bit about getting instructions right – 'Did I hear that properly?' 'Is that what she really said?' that kind of thing.

One of the things we had to do was deliver mail to the factory, and that was an experience I dreaded. There were hordes of fellas there. As well as making baby things, the factory used to make sanitary towels, and there were ladies working on the conveyor belts, putting the loops on, while the men did the heavy work, such as lifting the big bales of cotton wool. The place used to be covered in white fluff – wouldn't dare think what it did to their lungs. But the fellas used to throw sanitary towels at you, they'd land at your feet, and I used to feel physically sick when it was my turn to deliver mail into that sort of atmosphere.

The other thing was, the stench of where the baby cream was made used to make me want to throw up. So I don't know which was worse – the fear that made me want to be sick, or the smell of the baby cream.

After a very short time in the filing office, I moved to Accounts and became a Sunstrand machine operator. These were accounting machines, on the go long before computers. They were machines with ledger cards, so you did your sales ledger or your purchase ledger or your nominal ledger, all on a Sunstrand, on cards. My money went up, which was good. When I started, I got the princely sum of three pounds ten shillings a week, of which I had to give my sister one pound ten. I had two pounds left, but my sister insisted that I save half of that. So I had a pound left.

And what did that pound buy you?

Quite a lot, actually. When you think that two of you could go to the pictures and buy a big bag of Quality Street for ten shillings – a real good night out for ten shillings! And my fares to work were only thruppence each way on the bus so, when my money went up, it was okay. When I left, I was earning about five pounds a week, and that was good money.

Having gained the required experience I very quickly moved on, first working for a large organisation in the West End and later working for the Ford Motor Company near St Paul's in the City. My money had soared to the dizzy heights of forty pounds a month: the girl had arrived.

My sister had made me open a Post Office account, and when I had enough money saved she took me to Burnt Oak to buy clothes. Little did I realise then the significance of the area for Irish people. I knew nothing of Edgware at that time.

What about your first forays into social life?

My sister Marie was a lot livelier than Stasia, who was a bit staid. Marie must have been wondering what this poor girl – me – was doing apart from going to work and coming home again. So she decided to send me off with her neighbour's daughter, Sandra, to have a night out. We went to a dancing school in High Barnet called the North Twenty. I enjoyed the dancing lessons, but once the lights went down for the dancing proper, I'd escape to the cloakroom and wait for Sandra. I didn't have the courage to stand around and wait to be asked up. It was a bit of a trial.

But the girls at work were all lovely, although sometimes I felt a bit out of it. They took me once to a coffee bar in New Barnet run by a gay fella – in those days, they were called nancy boys. I had no idea in the name of God what a nancy boy was, so they took me off to the coffee bar, and there was this fella who pranced around with his bleached blonde hair – I'd never seen anything like it in my life. It was all very far from Mooncoin. I was gobsmacked.

We used to go and buy make-up on payday, too. One and six bought you pan-stick – as if we needed it, with perfect complexions; dear God, talk about putting it on with a trowel. And my friend Brenda and I used to wear this very pale pink lipstick and black eyeliner. She was my saviour, really; she taught me to jive behind the filing cabinets at work.

I went to my first all-night party at her house. It was only an all-night party because there was a bus strike and I wouldn't have been able to get back home. After great persuasion – and believe you me, it was difficult – my sister Stasia agreed to me going to this party. It was hell on earth trying to get permission for something like that.

In those days, things like that were just not allowed – girls going on holiday with their boyfriends, staying out at night. Anyway, this party was a totally innocent affair. My friend's parents were away on holiday in Rimini, and I remember thinking she was so far above me. Talk about exotic – Rimini for your holidays!

At the end of the night, when the party was over, the girls slept upstairs and the boys downstairs. All us girls washed our stockings before we went to bed. Girls always did that then – no such thing as putting stockings in a linen bin: they were always washed at night before you went to bed. And there was a hell of a battle in the morning, trying to sort out all the stockings in the bathroom.

Did you feel different from these girls because you were Irish?

I did, I did definitely. I didn't feel as *au fait* with everything as they did. In a lot of ways, I longed for Irish company. That came about through meeting a girl who was a friend of my sister Stasia. She was considerably older than I was, and my sister felt it would be all right for me to go off to an Irish dance with her. And, boy, that was the beginning of the good times! The first dance we went to was in the Round Tower in Holloway Road. Then I really found my feet and met other people. My sister used to go mad because I was out such a lot.

We used to go to the Gresham in Archway, the Blarney in Tottenham Court Road, the Galtymore in Cricklewood – there were Irish clubs all over the place in those days. To think that the only one to have survived out of all those Irish dancehalls is the Galtymore. The trolley-buses were still running then, and the 645 used to go to Cricklewood. It was grand getting down to Cricklewood, but it was a problem getting home.

It was the late 1950s before I really found my social feet. And bear in mind I was married in 1960. Once I found the Irish community, I was away. Mind you, I don't think I'd have liked to live in any of those areas, but it was lovely to go there and then come back home to Barnet, which I loved. It was a lovely place. I never felt I wanted to live in Cricklewood, or the Holloway Road – some of those places could be quite rough.

Once, outside the Round Tower, the police were called to break up a fight. But they just stood back and let the Irish fellas flog each other to death. They were probably quite wise; they used to do that a lot. They just moved in and picked up the pieces when it was all over. But these fellas decided that *nobody* was taking their mates away. They'd been killing them five minutes previously, but now they weren't going to let them be taken away, so they pulled the doors clean off the Black Maria.

I can see why my sister used to be worried. Some of the dancehalls could be rough, and these fellas would be well inebriated. They wouldn't come into the dance until late in the night; all us girls would have been sitting around the walls all evening like wallflowers, and then they'd come in, 'last knockin's'. And to be honest, I don't think that that has changed much.

Was there a lot of drinking?

With fellas, there was. Girls were a different kettle of fish. I had my pioneer pin before ever I left Ireland. But fellas, oh God yes, fellas drank. To be honest, looking at that now, a lot of that was loneliness. A lot of them came from big families and were now living on their own, in one room in Cricklewood. They went looking for companionship. And going to the pub five or six nights a week for companionship, the drink got a hold of them without them realising it.

They used to go to the pub straight from work in their dirty old clothes, and then the stereotype kicked in. English people used to see them wrapped around lampposts, spewing up after closing-time, and believe that that was what every Irish person was about.

I dissociated myself from that sort of behaviour. I'd have walked away from someone in Mooncoin behaving like that, so I dissociated myself from it here.

Was there a lot of subdivision within the Irish community?

Oh, yes, I would say that there were subdivisions, certainly. Mayo people always stick together. I have to say that they are exemplary in the way they look after each other. If one of them falls on hard times, the others will pull out all the stops to make sure that that person is cared for. I've seen situations in recent years where they'll hold a race night, for example, in order to raise money – and believe you me, there's big money going across the table. They're some of the nicest people I've ever met, salt of the earth. No bullshit. A lot of them now are millionaires, purely by hard work. They're real grafters.

Another one of the subdivisions was the Dubliners, who thought of the rest of us as culchies. A lot of us country girls, I would have to say, didn't like the Dublin crowd. The girls were a bit racy and ahead of us in a lot of ways. The Dublin fellas always had the reputation of being dirty fighters. Country fellas would give some bloke a good belting, but Dublin fellas would use bottles and stuff like that. They were renowned for it.

One night when I was in a club in Finsbury Park a row started, and, without a word of a lie, the Dublin girls went around collecting bottles for ammunition. All I wanted was to get out, to get home. It was a really serious fight.

Did all of your social life revolve around the Irish community, or did you have friends who were English?

For the most part, my social life was spent with Irish people, although I did have one English boyfriend. But before that, I have to tell you about the time I went out with a Connemara man! I met him at an Irish dance – for the life of me, I don't know which dance it was. Anyway, we agreed to go out.

By this time, I was working in the West End. There was a nice restaurant close to where I worked, and the girls and I used to go there sometimes for lunch. I thought it'd be a nice place to take him, but my Connemara man just sat there, slurping his soup, and the Lord save us, I never heard anything like it! I used to go in there fairly regularly, and I was beginning to feel a little bit embarrassed, to say the least!

We went to Mooney's in the Strand for a drink. Some fellow came in and my lad spotted him and followed him up to the bar. It must have been someone from Connemara, because the next thing is, the two of them have their arms around one another, slapping each other on the back, talking away in Gaelic.

Although I'd done Irish at school, I wouldn't have been able to join in the conversation. But that never arose, anyway. He was standing at the bar and I think he truly forgot that I was with him. I sat there for a while until I realised he wasn't coming back. So I got up from the table and walked out the door.

As I walked back to the Tube station, I kept looking back over my shoulder, but there was no sign of your man. So I reckon, about closing time, he must have looked around and asked himself 'Ah, Jaysus, where's the quare one gone?' I vowed and declared after that that I was never again going out with a Connemara man. I think the West of Ireland men had the reputation among us girls of being a bit 'culchie', a bit uncouth, like. We may have been totally wrong, but we were looking for something a little bit more refined!

Yes, I did have an English boyfriend once, and he was lovely. My friend Mary and I went to Barnet Fair together once – it's more like a big carnival than a fair, and it's held every year. I had to ask my sister's permission before I could go – it really wasn't the place for young ladies, as far as she was concerned.

On the day, Mary and I headed off down to the shops and bought ourselves some nice trousers – very tight: they were drainpipes in those days. This didn't meet with my sister's approval either, of course.

Nevertheless, we dressed up in our drainpipes and off we went to Barnet Fair. We were on the dodgems, and this lad kept bumping us. He started talking to us at the rifle range. When we got to the bus stop, he asked could he see me the following day. As it was Sunday, I had to tell my sister where I was disappearing off to – I couldn't tell her a lie. Well, there was this unholy row that I was going out to meet some fellow that had 'picked me up' at Barnet Fair!

I was in my bedroom crying when my brother Paddy arrived. By a strange coincidence, Paddy knew the boy's family and said to my sister 'Ah, will you let the girl go off, sure he's a grand lad.' I went off and met him, but my sister insisted I was back at half six. We couldn't go in to London, so we went for a walk in the park in High Barnet instead. He couldn't believe I had to be home so early. When he left me home he said 'It's the first time in my life I've ever taken a girl out and not spent a penny on her!' He was a lovely lad; his name was John.

We went out together for quite a while, but my sister was very, very disapproving. John was English and, worse than that, he was not a Catholic. She might have been able to cope with the fact that he was English, but she certainly couldn't cope with the fact that he was not a Catholic. He even came to Mass with me on Sundays to try and get in her good books, but he couldn't.

We'd sit on the bottom stair before he went off home, and my sister used to roar down at us from the top of the stairs 'Are you coming up here yet?' or 'Get away home with you, now!' He was a teddy-boy too, of course, which didn't endear him to her either. He wore the drainpipe trousers and the drape jacket and bootlace tie. He also had a lovely camel-coloured coat. Every time he wore it, my sister would say 'Here he comes in his bum-freezer!' He'd the DA hairstyle, too – a very handsome boy he was and generous to a fault. He'd spend all his money on me at the weekend and then phone me at work midweek and say 'If you've got ten bob on you, we can go to the pictures tonight!'

One night, my sister threw the brush at him from the top of the stairs, chasing him off home. He got sick of it all, eventually, and the relationship ended. That was the perception then – Catholic first, or nothing. At that time, the Church played very little part in my life. I took my faith for granted. I was a lot older before I grew to understand what my faith really meant to me, and by then I was married with two children.

What age were you when you got married?

I was far too young when I got married – barely nineteen. I suppose I saw marriage as an escape. My sister was much too strict; although, looking back I don't blame her. She had never had any children of her own, and suddenly she had a teenager who was just feeling her feet, out until all hours dancing. I used to dance three nights of the week – Friday, Saturday and Sunday – and maybe Sunday afternoons as well.

I can understand her worries, but we're now talking about more liberated times, getting towards the sixties. She was too strict. So marriage was definitely my way out of that. I was nineteen on the nineteenth of September and I got married on the twenty-fourth.

Like every youngster, the more adamant she was that I was not getting married, the more adamant I became that I was. I was by no means unusual – there were a lot of young marriages in those days, a lot of young people like me, all eager to make a life of their own. As young as we were, we had hopes and aspirations, we were madly in love, but of course the reality turned out to be a lot different to our expectations.

I met Larry in the Round Tower in Holloway Road, and you'd have stood in the snow to look at him. He was so handsome – tall, beautifully dressed. I can even remember what he wore: a dark suit, white shirt, red tie. We knew each other just thirteen months before we were married.

Larry had been brought up in Roscommon, again one of a big family. But he wasn't allowed to go to school if there was work to be done at home on the farm. God love him, he had very little education. I realise now, looking back, that he was probably dyslexic as well. When we were getting married, he had to practise signing his name in advance so that he could sign the register.

In the year before we married, there were signs of the jealousy and insecurity that were to cause so many problems later on. But I was in love, he was gorgeous and that's all you see when you're nineteen.

We got married at the Catholic church in Union Street, High Barnet. We held the reception in the Union Hall, with the catering done by the Co-op. The meal alone cost us fifty pounds not to mention the wedding cake and the drinks.

With both my parents dead, we had to finance the wedding ourselves. My sister would have no hand, act or part in that. She used to say to me 'If you marry that boy, you'll never need to say another act of contrition: your whole life will be one long act of contrition.' God love her, how right she was.

The whole day was great, and that afternoon Larry and I headed off on our honeymoon to Bognor Regis. Exotic! There was a big ruckus after we left, and I'm glad we weren't there. It was all drink fuelled, of course. Fortunately, my brother Paddy, who had given me away, took charge of the situation and the trouble makers were soon sent on their way.

After we were married for a while, we moved to Huntington, as part of Larry's job. My sister Anastasia had moved there too. But I never settled.

Was there any sense of gravitating towards an Irish community in this new place that you lived?

No. It was the only place I've ever lived where I felt that not only to be Irish, but to be a Catholic, was a distinct disadvantage. We were invited by the company Larry worked for to go and have a look at the new housing development while it was being built. They arranged a coach outing, and we were met by all the civic dignitaries – the Mayor and the Lady Mayoress, they were all there – and we had tea in the Town Hall.

I remember chatting to one of the dignitaries – I don't know which one, but somebody with a chain! I asked her if there was a Catholic church there, and she said 'Oh, yes, I believe there is one in the Hertford Road somewhere.' Then I asked her if there was a Catholic school nearby, because by this time I was pregnant. 'Oh, no, there's no Catholic school,' she said, very haughtily. 'When you come here, you're coming to Cromwell country.' I felt like hitting her. So I said 'Yes, he was the one who almost destroyed your monarchy, wasn't he?'

That was the welcome we got when we went to Huntington. Huntington was like Harlow in those days – a brand new town, just in the process of being built. There was no Irish community there whatsoever, apart from a few Irish families who had moved there like us. I felt very isolated. When we moved there, the roads weren't even made. I remember going to the doctor's, heavily pregnant by this stage. I was walking along this field, really, not yet a road, and I was wearing lace-up shoes. I got stuck in the mud and my foot came out of my shoe. So my foot landed in the muck and one of the guys who was working on the building site came to my rescue. He picked me up and carried me out of the mud.

I went home crying and asked my husband if he'd taken me there to bury me. I hated it. I hated every minute of it. We stayed for thirteen years.

My children were my saving grace; my life. And obviously I made a nice home for them. But I was not sad to leave there, I can assure you. As there was no Catholic school there, my sister Anastasia rented out the local hall and took it upon herself to give children religious instruction, and to prepare those who wanted to receive First Holy Communion. She was a good Catholic, a very good woman in so many ways.

After thirteen years in Huntington, did your sons feel Irish in any way?

I don't think so, no. They were aware that they had Irish parents, and they were used to hearing Irish music in the house, but they felt no big Irish connection. I don't think they ever felt the need to look for their roots – they were always quite content to be English.

We had one particularly wonderful holiday together in Ireland, the boys and I. Larry and I had split up at that stage. The boys were growing up by then, teenagers, and they loved Ireland and everything about it – the culture, the way of life. They really couldn't wait to go back. Even now, my son Ray loves it, although he doesn't get to go back very often. But he doesn't feel displaced here in England, not in any sense, not in the way some second-generation Irish do.

Where is home for you?

I find it a strange phenomenon that when I'm here I talk about going 'home' to Ireland, and when I'm 'at home' in Ireland, I talk about coming back here as 'going home'. I must admit there is a sense for me of not belonging totally in either place. Even though we have made a home here, 'home' is where we were born and where our heart is. Our hearts have never left there. I very often have the feeling of being neither one thing nor the other.

I think, too, that the longer you stay here the more difficult it is to make the break and go back to Ireland. That point in your life where it is possible suddenly passes. The problems begin once you've had your children and the children go to school. They start to make their friends, and you'd be loath to do anything that would change their lives, or to expect them to make changes for you. Because, at the end of the day, that's what you'd be doing – you'd be fulfilling your wishes, but disregarding theirs, if you decided just to up sticks and go back to Ireland.

And then there's the strange situation when they've flown the coop, and you think 'I can do it now: I can go back home to Ireland.' Before you know where you are, you've got grandchildren, and then you're pulled right back in again. You reach a point where you have to think 'Is it practical, for one thing?' and 'Do I really want now, at this stage of my life, to start all over again?'

I'm not sure, either, of how accepted one would be. I could feel just as isolated at home now as I did when I first came to London as a youngster. The welcome is lovely when you go home, and everything on holiday is wonderful, but the reality of living there could be something entirely different.

Ireland has moved on so much – economically, so many people have missed the boat for going home, as it were. Myself included. Ten or fifteen years ago, we probably would have been able to buy a property in Ireland, with money left over. But now, we've got to the stage where, economically, it wouldn't be such a good idea. We'd probably pay more for a property in Ireland than we would here. I would certainly consider moving out of London before we get too much older. In a way, that would provide a good compromise, as it would mean a gentler pace of life and all the benefits we now enjoy. Most of all it would mean I would be, at most, a few hours away from my son, my daughter-in-law and my grandchildren.

I'll be sixty on my next birthday, and I also have to be sensible from a health point of view. The health care here is very good. Would I have the same care in Ireland? Would I have to pay for it?

When you think about your 'heart home' rather than your 'made home' – to return to the distinction you made yourself – what is in that fantasy for you?

That's a tough one. I think, if I did go back, that I would not be able to live in the depths of the country again. Although I was brought up in the country, I am a city girl now, whether I like it or not. If I did go back, it would be into suburbia, or somewhere within easy reach of a city. I'd have withdrawal symptoms if I couldn't go to the theatre, if I couldn't be near some decent shops. I couldn't be somewhere where I felt very cut off; I couldn't live a very isolated life.

I don't know that I've ever really fantasised about an ideal situation for going home. I admire people who've had the courage to take the plunge and go, the same way I admired people who had to leave everything behind to come here, to England. I know people who have gone back, and the decision has worked very well for them. But equally, I know others for whom the reality has not lived up to the dream. In my case, I think it would be doubly difficult because my second husband, James, is an Englishman. Why would he want to spend the rest of his days in a foreign country? As he says 'Yes, you would be going home, but I would be leaving home.' Strangely enough, I've found that when an Irish person marries an English person, very often that English person loves Ireland and everything that goes with being Irish. And certainly James is no exception in that respect. He adores going to Ireland and loves the craic – but living there would be another matter. I've found that the English partners in relationships take on our history a lot more. They even defend our history, particularly during times when we've had troubles here. You hear people saying 'Bloody Irish, they're at it again.' And they start waffling on. Sometimes I've had to walk away myself, but my husband has often told people that they don't know what they're talking about. 'I've defended your corner,' he'll say to me. There's huge ignorance in England about Ireland and Irish issues, an enormous misconception in general. Sadly, the media play a large part in that misconception. With the best will in the world, people tend to believe the propaganda machine. Thankfully, the chickens-and-pigs-in-the-kitchen stories have finally been laid to rest.

What part, if any, did the Catholic Church play in your life in London?

When I was getting married at nineteen, my attitude to the Church was exactly as it had been when I left Ireland. Nothing had changed. In those days, you lived your life by what you were taught by the Church, and all that went with it. One of those things was birth control. The day before the wedding, both Larry and I went to confession because we wanted to be in a state of grace before we went to the altar.

Then we went to Oxford Street, to pick up my wedding ring. As we would be going off on honeymoon the following day, we decided we had better get some 'things', you know? We stood outside the chemist, going from one foot to the other, deliberating as to how we were going to go in and ask for these 'things', which obviously neither of us had ever done before. We were trying to work out before we went in how many we'd need. And we said, well, we're going away for a fortnight, so that's fourteen days, multiplied by … anyway, we somehow arrived at three dozen. Don't ask me how we worked it out, but we did.

Larry plucked up the courage to ask for the Durex, but the fella behind the counter couldn't understand what we meant, so we had to spell it out for him. It was bad enough plucking up the courage to ask for them in the first place, but then we had to insist that we wanted *thirty-six*. I don't think he was winding us up, I think he was genuinely taken aback that we wanted thirty-six in one go.

And to be honest with you, I don't think we used them all, and we never bought any more. We were petrified, sick at having to go in and ask for them, particularly as we had just come from confession. Here we were now, flying in the face of God. Buying them was the worst; using them wasn't all that bad.

And although I was happy with the decision not to have a baby immediately, I'd have to say that it worried me in terms of my faith. Then, after I'd had two boys within eighteen months, the doctor warned me not to get pregnant again for several years. I went on the pill, and that was the real trauma. I had many sleepless nights before I went to confess my sin. When I think of it now! As luck would have it, I got a very understanding priest in confession, so it was easier after that. And it was just as well – the marriage was already proving to be unsatisfactory in quite a lot of ways. I think I mightn't have left the marriage if I'd been living at home in Ireland. The fact that we lived here did give us more control over our lives. We were several years ahead of life at home in Ireland in that respect.

In a small community, there isn't the anonymity that you have here. At least here, if you were in a bad marriage, you could walk away if there wasn't any other answer. People don't poke into your life the way they would at home. For instance, if I'd been in Ireland I wouldn't have had the nerve to speak up to the priest in the way I did, and, if I'd already left, I probably would have gone back.

I was living apart from my husband, and he sent this priest to see me. The priest proceeded to tell me that, in my situation, I was one step down from the gutter. I should go back, hand in hand with my husband and my children, and that that was the only way I would ever find true happiness. Unfortunately, he got an earful back. I felt he needed to be told straight and fair that he didn't know what he was talking about. I feel that that incident could have turned me against the Church – maybe that's not true, but it certainly turned me against priests like him. I was very fortunate to meet someone very shortly after that who was a lovely man, the parish priest of where I was living in Rickmansworth. He was totally understanding about my decision to leave my husband. He reassured me that, if it had happened in his parish, he'd have advised me to leave. My main concern was for my children's happiness. I also wanted to give them the best opportunity I could to secure a better future. And Rickmansworth offered them that better future – I had moved because there was nothing for them in Huntington. We became great friends, Fr Lemmon and I. He brought my case to Westminster, to have my marriage annulled. I also met another lovely priest through him, Fr Tom O'Brien, and he has stayed in my life ever since. He was involved with the Scouts there, he became a great friend of my children, and, subsequently, he was the one to bury my son Laurence after he was killed in a car accident. He also married my elder son, Ray. He has been a real source of comfort to me down the years. I think religion was a matter of location, in some ways. Here, it was a very different thing from at home in Ireland. I felt that here people went to Mass of their own accord, whereas at home, in those days, people went to Mass because they would have been talked about if they didn't.

I suppose that, during my earlier years, the Church attended to my spiritual needs, but not much outside that. I think that the Church could have been a lot more proactive; they could have played a much more important role in people's lives, in making them feel more at home here, and maybe even giving them some guidance in practical things. I think their only preoccupation was with our spiritual needs, when in fact some people were just hanging on in there by the seat of their pants. There wasn't too much worry about how they were getting on with their daily lives. The Church could have had a greater influence in that situation.

There is a sense in which those young people who arrived here in the fifties had to grow up very quickly, very thoroughly. Was that your experience?

Yes. Definitely. You had to. To be honest, I think people of our generation grew up more quickly anyway. People left home younger because they had to, and there wasn't the degree of mollycoddling then that there is today. Coming here, you had to get streetwise pretty quickly. Things like finding your way around, knowing where to go and where not to go, how to behave, even. You had to take responsibility for looking after yourself in a big city, and sometimes that meant, as in my case, that you never drank alcohol.

We became adults overnight. I regret the speed of that. I have no regrets about getting married, because out of that marriage I had two wonderful children. I wouldn't change one thing about that.

At the time, I don't think I felt that I was missing out on anything. I absolutely loved that time with my children, absolutely loved it. I was at home full time. It was all fulfilling; they were all I ever dreamed of. It was later on, when the children started to grow up a bit – when I didn't have to be there for them twenty-four hours a day – that I felt a little bit cheated that I hadn't had more time when I was younger, and that I had missed out on things.

When I got divorced from my first husband, and became older and wiser, I did make up for that in *some* ways. I did enjoy my life, and I did go out more, but, having said that, I've always been happiest when I've had somebody to look after.

What stage was your career at during those times? Had you re-entered the workforce?

I'd been back in the workforce ever since my children were small. I started to work part time in a hotel. I didn't go back just for the money I could earn. I went back for my survival. The marriage was decidedly rocky, and I felt I had no way out. Going out and getting a little job gave me back my confidence, which had been in tatters. It worked wonders for me.

After that, I worked locally, in two different offices. Once the children were at school, I was back at work full time. I was on the PTA of my children's school, and I remember the headmaster asking me if I would consider teacher training. I must admit, I would have loved to do it at that point, but it would have been difficult to give up a paid job to go into teacher training.

Was there ever a stage in your life here when you found it uncomfortable to be Irish?

I don't know that I felt uncomfortable in the early days. Certainly I felt a bit isolated at times, lonely at times, but not uncomfortable.

But, when the Troubles at home heated up a bit and transferred here, it did become uncomfortable. Hand on my heart, I've never ever felt ashamed to be Irish, but there were times when I didn't want to shout it from the rooftops. You'd be on your way to work in the mornings, and you'd pick up a newspaper and there it was, emblazoned across the front page: some awful atrocity, like Harrods. People were disgusted by it. Irish people here were disgusted by it and did not want in any way to be associated with it. A lot of English people were very understanding about that, I have to say. They understood that it was only a minority. But it did make you hang your head a bit.

Those were some very hard times here for the Irish, with people pulled in who had nothing to do with these things. When atrocities happen like that, heads will roll, and the authorities had to be seen to be doing something. Sadly, as we now know, this resulted in many wrongful convictions.

There has been a great interest here in the Peace Process. I support those who were brave enough to take that step. I think they are greatly to be admired, no matter what side of the divide they come from. People are very keen to see the Process work, and there have been a lot of prayers for peace, certainly in our church. Ireland has been torn apart long enough; none of us here, or at home, wants to see it go on any longer. Everybody wants to see it end.

Do you still go back to Ireland regularly?

I do indeed, as often as my friends will have me! The country has moved on light years from the Ireland that I left – the changes really delight me. It's now an extremely prosperous country. In a lot of ways, I feel that Ireland had a lot of catching up to do, and it's doing that now, and it's rightly deserved. It's great, thanks be to God. Not so many people are forced to leave now – they don't have to do what the likes of us did. They can make a living at home, they can have their own homes and they *can* stay in their own country and bring up their children. I'm delighted for them that they can do that. I'm glad that they don't have to experience the heartbreak of taking the boat.

It's still something that makes me very sad.

'EVERY TIME I LEAVE ENNIS A BIT OF ME DIES'

Kevin Casey is a born communicator, a man who radiates energy and intelligence. Now in his early seventies, Kevin has been living and working in and around London for over fifty years.

I think it's safe to say that you had a most unusual job when you came to London first. Can you tell me about it?

Before I left Ireland, I worked in Ennis in the Old Ground Hotel. It was a wonderful place to work because it was associated with Shannon. The Americans, at that time, were coming into the Old Ground Hotel, coming back to Ireland, as they say. The world was coming in and out of this little market town called Ennis, and it was great! We had Pan American, Transocean Airlines, American Overseas Airlines – and the man whose family owned the Old Ground, Brendan O'Regan, he became the kingpin for Shannon. He's now Doctor Brendan O'Regan. His family was great to work for. He started off the Duty Free in Shannon, the first Duty Free in the world.

I was twenty years old at the time. It happened that work in the Old Ground became very seasonal, so Brendan O'Regan asked me would I like to have a go at being a valet, as he knew some Lord in England. What did I know about valeting? But I said, sure I'd have a go. I'm that kind of fellow anyway. So I went to work for this Lord, and I had a lovely life entirely. His name was Lord Beatty, a man of Irish origin. His father was Admiral Beatty who'd served in the 1914–18 War. The son is known as Viscount Borrodell, and Borrodell is in Cork, I think. When you look back on the history of the Beattys, the grandparents had their own army in Ireland.

But I had a great time working for the man, travelling up and down to London, to the Ritz Hotel, all that sort of thing. We lived in a village called King's Sutton, just outside Banbury, and it was usual for top personalities to call and stay. I met David Niven, Jack Warner, Jennifer Jones, David O. Selznick, Princess Radziwill – these were the people who used to stay with Lord Beatty. It was a great adventure.

I remember going to a pub one night in King's Sutton, and it was full of people. In the crowd was this chap wearing a little shamrock badge. It was what was known as the Aer Lingus badge. I went over to him and asked him was he Irish. 'I am,' he said, 'from Tipperary.' He was a groom from one of the other estates, and we became great pals. It's not that the people from the village weren't sociable – they were, and they made us very welcome. But there's something about looking for your own identity, your own language, your own accent. It's something to home in on, something familiar.

Holding onto your religion is very important in terms of your identity, too. I remember Lord Beatty came to me one day and said 'I believe you're going to leave me, Kevin.' And I replied 'I have to, my Lord. My religion is very important to me.' At that time, it looked as though there would be a conflict between my duties and going to Mass on Sundays.

He asked me what time I went to my Church, and I said about half-past nine. He said he couldn't see the problem. I said 'You have a lot of guests here, my Lord, at weekends, and I have to help out.' His reply was 'Well, they'll just have to wait for their breakfast until you come back.' He never stood in my way at all as regards my religion.

That's a fact.

Did you try at any stage to come back to Ireland, to look for work at home again?

I did. When I'd had enough of that job, I came back to Ireland. I was over two years with Lord Beatty and I came back to Ireland on holidays. That was in the early fifties. I started to look around for something. My brother's wife came down to visit me, and she had her cousin with her. I fell in love with the cousin, and she's now my wife, Kathleen. She was nursing over here in St Stephen's Hospital in Fulham. She'd started her nursing in Guildford in Surrey when she was seventeen and then she moved to St Stephen's. I told Kathleen I'd meet her back in London the following week. She never thought I would, but I did. I went back, and I never looked for work in Ireland again. I got a job in a bar in London, in the Brazen Head in Marylebone. I went in as a barman and finished up as a manager.

This was a complete contrast to the life I'd led up to that. From the Ritz Hotel to being a publican, meeting the Irish coming in – it was a huge change. These men used to stay in digs, but digs didn't want you there in the evenings. The Irish in those days were so grateful to have somewhere to go. At three o'clock, they were out on the streets again. And there weren't the amount of cafés and restaurants that there are now. In the evening, they'd go back to their digs in Kilburn and Maida Vale, or wherever they were.

That was why the pub became a ghetto system, perhaps, a community of sorts. Those men used to say to me 'Why won't the Catholic Church over here build hostels for us?' Well, my experience has been that there are two Catholic Churches. The English Catholic and the Irish Catholic weren't the same people at all. Their attitudes were totally different. The Irish Catholic was the poor relation of the English Catholic. Don't forget that the relationship between England and Ireland wasn't always the greatest.

But I also believe that the Irish government had a responsibility to those men, and so did the Catholic Church in Ireland – from the day they made their First Holy Communion. But once they stepped on the boat to Holyhead, it was 'Amen, goodbye, thank God our unemployment figures are down.' Nobody wanted to know. I feel very angry over that.

I often asked these men why they'd left their families. And they'd say 'Kevin, they're better off without me.' Some of them became alcoholics. They weren't fit for work. And then they got out of the way of working. It was very sad. We often gave them food that was left over from the bar.

A lot of the Irish around London at that time depended on the Salvation Army hostels. And they were very, very basic indeed. You'd to be in at a certain time, and out at a certain time in the morning. Either you had a job, or you walked the streets. Some men used to stay in those hostels until they had saved enough money to go home again to Ireland.

I saw a lot of Irish girls come over, too. I'm not going to judge anybody, perhaps they would have gone that way even at home, but they ended up on the streets. I remember speaking to one of the girls and telling her I was going back home on holidays. She gave me money and asked me to give it to her father. 'Tell him I'm working for Walls,' was what she said. 'Don't tell him what I'm doing.' And that was sad. Very sad. There was no support for those girls, same as with the Irish navvy. No support at all.

The Irish had a hard-drinking, hard-fighting reputation, and we were all painted with the same brush. I remember once going out with an English girl and she said to me 'My family are not very keen for me to go with you, because they think there'll be a houseful of children. You're a Catholic.' That's how they saw you. It's very hard to blame people for that. If that's the image they're given of the Irish, that's the image they'll have.

My wife, Kathleen, was a nurse, and you'd need to see the dedication of the Irish to the nursing profession. There seemed to be a different attitude towards the nursing profession. They were a very accepted body of people.

But in general, when we Irish came over here we felt we weren't wanted. Still, one of the differences I saw between the Irish and other groups was that the Irish went to work and became involved. They got involved in the unions and did very well there. People asked why, and the answer is because the Irish were always fighting for justice. They came out of a country that was looking for justice for hundreds of years. And Irish people arrived here well aware that they were the foreigners, the outsiders. They had no illusions about England being the Mother Country. Others came from the Commonwealth, the West Indians feeling that they were owed a living. They'd been told that this was their country, that they were British. The Irish had no such expectations.

Nowadays, you have educated men coming out of Ireland. It's a very different experience for them.

You say that all the Irish were painted with the one brush. Did you experience any anti-Irish sentiment during your long career in England?

No, I didn't. I was very fortunate in that regard. There was only one occasion, when I worked in a factory – I finished my days in a factory. A chap came to me, and he was on about the IRA. 'Excuse me,' I said, 'would you repeat what you've just said?' He repeated whatever it was he had said, and I said to him 'Look, let's go up to the Personnel Officer and you can ask him the same thing in front of me. Then, I'll get the Plant Manager in and you can say the same thing in front of him. After that,' I told him, 'we can go to the Race Relations Board and you can say the same thing to them. Are you associating me with some organisation of which I know nothing? You seem to know all about them.'

He tried to say it had been a joke. 'No jokes,' I said. 'That's the end of it now, son,' I said. 'My name is not Pat. My name is Kevin. You're John and I'm Kevin.'

If you didn't stamp your authority like that, your identity, everywhere you went, they'd walk on you. You had to be very strong. Thousands of Irish people will tell you the same thing. You had to be assertive. You had to stand up for yourself. Men who went into the forces had a terrible time with the dogmatic attitudes there. 'Oh, here comes more of the IRA' – this from men with stripes on their shoulders. And you couldn't answer back, not like in civilian life. They gave the Irish a dog's life.

But thousands and thousands of ordinary Irish people rose above those attitudes. They were hard workers, grafters, and they rose above it all. They became contractors and such like. What was always accepted was that Irish people built the roads, built the highways, so they were able to get involved in those businesses. Ninety per cent went up the hill, ten per cent down the hill. The vast majority worked hard. It was very tough work. And after a long day, they had nowhere to come back to, as such, except the camps. I remember those camps very well. You'd have to be made of very strong stuff to survive them.

I remember people at the train station in Ennis with labels on their lapels, on the way to the building industry in England. An agent brought them over, and for every one that he delivered to McAlpine, or whoever the builder was, he got paid. I saw them queuing up for the train that would take them to Holyhead.

There was a lot of misery left behind in those days. Perhaps we're not as angry as we could be because we did well ourselves.

Did you find that Irish people assimilated well, or did they want to retain their own identity?

They wanted to retain their own identity. I believe that of all the nationalities to enter Britain, the Irish are the slowest to settle. There was a study done some years ago on the amount of Irish that had died very young. A lot of them never married, so they were found in rooms, dead for days, and nobody even knew who they were. A lot of them were reluctant to marry because they had no security. They moved from job to job, increasing their lack of security.

I think marriage frightened many of them, too, perhaps from what they had seen at home. Too many children – they'd had to get out of those houses. And now there are so many single men, old men, with nowhere to go anymore. The clubs are gone, the pubs are different, the whole society is very different.

They can't even go home. So many of them lost touch with family in Ireland over the years. 'I've nothing to go back to,' they'd say. 'Nobody wants me. They don't want to see me – they want to see the colour of my money.' Brothers and sisters don't want them; nieces and nephews don't want to know. 'What are you doing here? Why don't you go back to England?'

And once the mother died, once there was no longer a mother in the house, there was no point in going back. This is another area where the Irish government could have done a lot more. I think that things are changing now, in 2003, and I know that the Aisling project has been set up to help bring some of these unfortunate men back home.

This is a strange thing about nationalities – people often comment about Polish people 'Why is their English so bad?' Do you know why they never picked up the English language? *Hoping to go home to Poland.* They didn't want to become too anglicised, too assimilated into another culture. Communism wouldn't let them go home for years.

Now that the time is here when they can go back, they're too old.

What do you believe to be the attitude of the Irish in Ireland to the returning emigrant?

The old cliché in Ireland when you were there on holidays was 'When are you going back?' The agenda was 'When are you going back, because you're not here to take my job, are you?'

I've met people who've gone back to live there, people who were not let settle back in. Not in jobs, nor anything else. The attitude was totally different. 'Now you're no longer an Irishman' – or 'Don't go bringing your English ideas over here' – that was the attitude. I've known men who went back to Ireland with modern ideas, better ideas – how to speed a job up, to make it safer, less labour-intensive. And what were they told? 'Never mind your English ideas over here, Paddy. Go back, we don't want you. We'll do things our way. Our ways, our problems.'

They didn't want to know. The returning emigrant no longer fitted into that community. Perhaps some did, but the overwhelming impression was that once you'd stepped on that boat – no matter how long you'd been in England or how short a time – you were different. If you came back as a single man, you were looked on with suspicion. 'You're not here to take my job.' Maybe one of the daughters or the sons wanted the farm or the house. Coming back as a single man, they thought 'Are you a danger to me, to my bringing in a husband, to my keeping the house?' There were all those hidden agendas. Of course there were.

And the fact that they weren't let settle in jobs if they did go home to Ireland – that goes way back to when I was a child in Ennis. This man used to walk down our road (I lived in a place called Clanroad). I asked my mother who he was. 'Oh, that's Old Doyle, the Yank,' she said. He was no longer an Ennis man. And the same happened to those who had been in England. You weren't even considered Irish anymore. You could feel it. There's an awful lot of begrudgery in Ireland. But people never said 'No' to the money that was going back all over the years, even long before the fifties. People working in the post office could tell you that – the money was sent back regularly, same as the American money was relied on when we were kids.

No matter how often I went back and forwards, nobody ever asked me what I was doing in England. You could be a pen-pusher up in Dublin with a greasy arse to your trousers, and people would say 'Oh, he's a civil servant, you know.' Great respect. You could be the Prime Minister of England, and it doesn't mean … *that*. You could be a Monsignor out in Africa doing Trojan work in schools, and nobody mentions it. Be a Parish Priest out in Lissycasey, and that's a different matter.

But I'm not bitter. I've no time for that.

I do know that pensioners in Ireland are treated really well, with travel allowance, fuel allowance, television and telephone allowances. It's a much better system for pensioners than it is here. It's disgraceful what they get away with here. The English are a very complacent nation. They allow us to play the Irish National Anthem after dances here – have done for years, going back to the sixties. We can fly our flag. But we were never a threat, and we built this town. When we book the big hall for our St Patrick's night dance – two hundred people, big bands – we decorate the whole place in green, white and gold. We could sell three hundred tickets!

You moved out of London when your family was young. Why was that?

My son Gerald was two and a half years old when we moved to Harlow. It was a new town then. In 1957, you could get a house in Harlow to go with your job. At that time, I was a glass-bottle inspector, and I then moved into quality control. I was with the same factory for thirty-seven years – United Glass. Not a lot of Irishmen went into factories. They preferred the identity of being on the buildings because they all knew each other. There was a closeness there, a clanship. And living here, you tend towards that sort of community living. Look at Kilburn, at the Irish papers where you can find out what's going on at home. I never lived in Kilburn myself; I came straight from Marylebone to Harlow.

Harlow in the fifties was a huge Irish community because of all the building that was going on. The town was in the middle of being built back then. There were five parish churches in this town. I got into the factory, got on well, worked hard, had my home and my three children educated, so England has been a very good country to me and to the thousands like me. No one ever stood in the way of my promotion or getting on.

Leave the politics out of your job. Leave the religion out of your job. No one ever stood in my way in that regard either. I was on twelve-hour shifts at one time, and I went to the manager and told him I had to go to Sunday Mass. 'No problem,' he said. 'Clock in and clock out and I'll sign your card when you come back.' No one stood in my way with regard to my religion. Other people will tell you different, but that was my experience.

Often, people blame the English for a lot of problems. But it wasn't a bed of roses among the Irish either. Take the ganger-men. They had a little bit of power. If your face didn't fit, you weren't picked up in the lorry in Kilburn the following morning. Sometimes, a man would be taken out on a job and the ganger-men took a dislike to him. They'd just dump him in the street and tell him to 'find your own so-and-so way home'. They were often paid in pubs, too. If you didn't buy your drink, you wouldn't be picked up the following day either.

How do your own children see their identity?

The older they got, the more Irish they became. The eldest boy especially. He loved the freedom of the farm when we'd go over on holidays to Kathleen's place. Today, he feels very Irish. The younger boy is the same, now. Perhaps not as much as Gerald, but he has become very Irish, too. Then there's my daughter. She liked London and she liked the community around the Church in London. Like all my children, she went to a Catholic school, and she liked that identification with the nuns. That sense of identity does matter. People say it doesn't matter, but it does; it matters an awful lot. For my children to be Catholic, to go to

Catholic schools, to know that their Dad is a member of the Knights of St Columba – that's all very important to a sense of identity.

I don't believe my children ever felt any prejudice because of being Irish. There were several nationalities in the Catholic schools they attended – Polish, English, Irish. I think they were very fortunate in that. I was always very much involved in the social side of things – organising dances and things like that. We kept the kids involved, and they liked to come to them. Obviously, being young boys and girls growing up, they had their own scene, but even now we still keep the Irish dances going as much as we possibly can. A lot of people love it.

I never shoved republicanism down my children's throats. I played my Irish music, they played theirs. They came to some of the Irish dances and enjoyed them, but children must find their own level.

Was the local Catholic church always a big part of your life?

Oh, yes. Most certainly yes.

The Catholic Church started these Catholic clubs, associated with the parish. They were great social centres. Marvellous places, great communication there. They were places to meet, families came in, there were dances. Irish dancing was promoted through these clubs as well. Year in, year out, for a long, long time. If anybody was sick, or needed a couple of hundred pounds to go back to Ireland or to bury somebody, it was there. Men who came into the town to build would head straight for the Catholic church, because they knew there would be a club there. It was somewhere to go, away from the digs.

Those clubs cleared the debts of many a church but, the sad thing was, they closed them down. As soon as they had finished with them, they turned the key and closed them. They no longer wanted that sort of club in their parish. 'Off you go now, lads, the debt is paid, and we don't want to be known as a drinking club any longer.'

It shocked a lot of the Irish. It happened in this town. We opened the Club here in Holy Cross in 1968, and it kept going until the eighties. Irish culture was kept alive through the Club: there were bands and celebrations for St Patrick's night and New Year's Eve, all the different events were kept going all the time. There was a great warmth of welcome for all, English and Irish, Catholic and non-Catholic. So it was an awful shock to the system when they closed the Club. The powers that be, whoever they are, closed the clubs once the church's debt was paid. That happened all over the country. Some are still going, but not nearly as many as before. It turned people off the Church, unfortunately.

Are you still involved in your local community?

Oh, yes, most certainly. Through the church, I do readings – the Lessons, that kind of thing. And I'm very active with the Knights. The Knights of St Columba was founded in 1919, in Glasgow. Men were coming back from the War, and they wanted a sense of identity. There was already an organisation in the United States called the Knights of St Columbus. All came from St Columcille. So in Glasgow, the organisation was founded on the basis of Charity, Unity and Fraternity.

The feeling was that the more we are together after the War, as a group of men, the more we can help each other. If one knows where there's a job going, or another hears where there's a bit of work going, they could help each other out. That community spirit was a big thing, and that's how the Knights of St Columba got started. There are different Councils, as we call them, right across the country. We organise lots of local events – for example, for children who are down and out.

Basically, anybody who needs a bit of help, the money is there for them. Wells for Water in Africa was a tremendous project we took up for the millennium year. You can sink a well in Africa for £10 and give people clean water. We raised £277,000 nationally for that. There are also on going collections for the Mother Teresa homes in India and for Romania.

I know we've been criticised for the fact that the Knights is an organisation reserved for Catholic men only. The general consensus is that we'd like to have women in it, but people in the North of England want to stick to the old routine – men only. Women help out on sub-committees, to organise things in conjunction with us, and they have often complained that the rules don't allow them to join. There's no secrecy to our organisation – all this about the freemasonry of the Catholic Church is hugely exaggerated. The only secret bit about the Knights of St Columba is when we want to do a charitable work. If we want to give someone some money, they become a number. They are protected by their anonymity. All our initiations are done in the Catholic church, openly, at Mass, so that everyone knows what's going on. Before a man joins, he is allowed to come into the order and see what we do at our meetings. We have a Grand Knight, a deputy Grand Knight, a Chancellor, Action Convenor, Secretary and so on. The collars are slowly being done away with – the full regalia is only worn at certain ceremonies. So the formality is slowly disappearing.

We take on a lot of social projects, like supporting the hospices this year. But we need more members. We live in a society today where people don't want to commit themselves. They won't go into the priesthood, they won't become nuns – it's very hard to get commitment from people because society is changing so completely. Those of us who started the Knights in Harlow in the sixties, we're all getting on now. We're all in our seventies. The good Lord calls a lot of us – we've lost three or four men in the last two years through cancer. That's very sad.

*You have a long history of involvement in Harlow, and this has been
your home for over forty years. Can you tell me what you think when
you hear the word 'home'?*

You never go on holidays when you're Irish. 'When are you going
home?' is always the question. Even our own children ask 'Are you
going home this year, Dad?'

Every time I leave Ennis a bit of me dies.

I would love to go home to Ireland. I haven't changed in that.
But house prices changed – an increase of £25,000 a year! They're
moving the goal posts on us all the time. I know that things have
changed a lot in Ireland. And the Dublin fellows here often say to
me 'Sure, you'd know no one, Kevin.' But that's not my experience.
I can go down the town, and everybody knows me. I was in Paddy
Quinn's pub in Ennis one night, and people were reminiscing.
Someone asked me had I worked in The Old Ground.

And of course, I had – in 1948. I used to love listening to the
Americans in those days. 'There's more to this world than what the
Christian Brothers told us' – that's what I used to think when I heard
them talk about this part of America and that part of America. One
day one of them said to me 'Red' – I had red hair at that time – 'don't
go hanging around this hotel too long. Don't finish up like Dennis,'
he said. 'He's an old man now. Get out into the world and see
something and meet some more people. Don't stay here.'

We used to have people come up to the Old Ground Hotel,
married women especially, with families. They'd sit there in the
lounge and ask 'Any Americans in, Kevin? Can we see them? Can
we see where they sleep?'

I went to the manager and I told him what they were looking for.
'Oh, show them around, Kevin,' he said. I took them around and
showed them the Americans' bedrooms, and then I'd bring them
back to the lounge and offer them tea and cakes, on the house.

So, years later, while we were reminiscing that night in Quinn's
Pub in Ennis, a woman asked me 'Kevin, what was all that about?'

'I'll tell you what,' I said. 'America was coming back to Ennis.'

These women had seen all their relations – aunts, cousins, sisters, brothers – go and never come back. And they were trying to identify *them* by looking at these American faces. And that is a fact. Some of them cried, grieving for the people who would never come back. They couldn't afford to come back. And there was nothing to come back to.

In my situation in Ennis in those days, I needed to move out. My mother was getting on in years. I knew the house would never be mine: my sister had married in there, so I knew that I had to move out. I wanted to go, too. I knew there was more money in England.

And that was the experience of so many young men and women in that decade: get out.

Why didn't I go back in the sixties when jobs were plentiful in Ireland? I was now established in a factory with a pension and the children's education was secure, so it was very difficult to leave. Some did, but I said no. The glassworks provided steady work, guaranteed money; there was overtime there. I never had a car in my life – never needed one. I cycled to work and cycled home. If I had to, there was public transport, or I could have walked. Kathleen used to walk to work, up to Marks and Spencer, and walk home again. Where we live is very central to the church and the shops and everything else. I couldn't possibly, with three children, take that risk of going back to Ireland. I didn't want to.

If the industries had been in Ennis before my children went to secondary school, then yes, I'd have taken a gamble then. Kathleen would have got a job as a nurse – yes, it would have been possible then. But that didn't happen. And if I couldn't go back to Ennis, I might as well stay here.

My town, my place was where I'd want to go back to. Not just 'Ireland'. And you can't regret that opportunity not having been there. Otherwise, you'd be like the pendulum of a clock, not belonging here, not belonging there, swinging back and forth. You must become established.

My wife and I belong here. We fit in. The Irish got involved. They didn't get into crime. They got involved in work and built their homes around them. They established their children. Children must be given security.

Both Kathleen and I have kept in constant touch with Ireland, with all our relations. I have only one sister left. Out of a family of nine, there's now only two of us. Kathleen has brothers and nieces and nephews in Ennis. We were fortunate in a lot of ways. And the children love going back to Ireland.

I'm an hour's journey from Stansted to Shannon, and then I'm back with my nephews and nieces. I love going back.

Do you feel in any way angry at the state that was responsible for the economic conditions that forced so many to emigrate?

Yes, I do. I certainly do.

I remember being in Limerick Junction one time when I'd gone back to Ireland and I picked up a newspaper there. It was the time 'Tayto' first came out. It made the owner a multi-millionaire – very clever man he was, too. I remember the headline about a speech by Seán Lemass: 'I will bring all the Irish back from England.' I didn't understand much about politics then, to be honest, not as much as I do now. But I don't think I blamed anybody in particular.

I remember questioning in later years whether Ireland shouldn't have remained part of the Empire. Would they have been better off to use the Empire? Would that have brought more business into Ireland? But politics is a very complex subject. Unless you understand all the whys and wherefores, it's easy to make the wrong decisions.

Do you see many changes in Ireland?

I do. Sadly so. I wish people would hold onto their religion. It's an identity. All the scandals within the Catholic Church have hurt me deeply. The real scandal is that all the genuine people within the Church are being hurt – all the priests and nuns and brothers. Really genuine people – the priests, so many of them Irish, who built schools and churches in new towns all over England. You've only got to pick up a magazine to see the work these people are doing in Africa on the missions out there. Jesus Christ was surrounded by people who denied him. If you feel you don't belong in the Church, get out of it.

There should never have been the big cover-up that's alleged to have gone on. That's hypocrisy. I would prefer to go to Mass once a month and know the priest was genuine. If a cover up is going on, then it's wrong. People should be vetted more before they become priests, psychologically and every other way. When people turn their back on the Church, maybe they have very good reason. It's all very, very sad.

Irish society has become very greedy. All the conversations I come across are about money – it's all money, money, money. They got money too fast. It will level out, but it will take another five or six years. Europe will have to pull on the reins and say 'Slow down – you're going much too fast.' Look at the suicide rates. Look at the deaths on the roads. It's appalling. But moral standards all over the world have sunk so low that people are afraid even to go into teaching. They're terrified even to put a hand on someone. The pendulum has swung far too far in the other direction.

I remember back in the forties and fifties people would stand and talk. Now nobody has the time to do that anymore. They're in their cars and they're gone. Why is there so much disunity in Ireland? What caused it?

Hang onto your identity. Holding onto your personal history and your language is so important. 'Ah, don't bother about all that,' they say to me. 'The Famine is over.' I don't want people to live in the past, but they're not willing anymore even to *talk* about their history.

When you look back over the forty years you've spent in London, what are the most significant things to have happened to you – things which perhaps wouldn't have happened had you stayed in Ireland?

Self-assurance.

The Christian Brothers beat it out of us. I found a lot of class distinction in the Christian Brothers. If you were a Garda's son, or a doctor's son, or a civil servant's son, there was a different attitude towards you. And you were never allowed to express an opinion. Not anywhere. The priest would come and speak to you if you spoke out. That's why when I met the Americans in the Old Ground I found it was like opening a gate into another world. There was such freedom of speech – men were talking openly, treating you as an equal. You weren't a servant, or a night porter – you were a person.

Even when I worked for Lord Beatty for two and a half years, I was treated as an equal. In fact, there was more class distinction among the servants than there was with Lord Beatty.

I'll tell you a funny story. One of the O'Briens of Dromoland Castle used to visit Lord Beatty. One day, he turned to me and said 'I believe you come from Clare, Kevin.' I said 'I do, I come from Ennis.'

'Wonderful!' he said. 'Do you know Dromoland Castle?'

'Yes,' I said. 'I do, I know it very well.'

'Oh,' he said, 'you must know my brother, Lord Inchiquin.'

'Of course he does,' interrupted Lord Beatty, 'he knows him very well! Will you come on – don't embarrass the boy!'

'Oh,' says O'Brien, 'I didn't mean it like that.'

But it was funny – they had no consciousness of class, not in the way I had experienced it in the Christian Brothers.

What I didn't tell O'Brien was that I did know Lady Inchiquin. She used to come to the Old Ground Hotel, in her great big station wagon. Trays and trays of chickens used to come from Dromoland Castle, brought to us by Lady Inchiquin herself.

How are your children's lives here different from what they might have been, had you stayed in Ennis?

My nephew once said to me 'What I like about the boys who moved out of Ennis in the 1950s is that they were the ones with spirit. They wanted to make something of their lives.' Mind you, the ones who stayed behind – when Seán Lemass opened things up – they did well. But that's another experience.

I've always been very strict on my family: my children had to make it here. And I'd got to make sure as their father that they made it. Their mother was strict with them, too. We had to be. I said to my sons that we had to do well; we had to get on with our jobs. There was no back door. There was nothing to go back to.

'Never mind that man standing in front of you at school. The schoolteacher doesn't care whether you do your books or not. He's got his profession. You've got to get yours through listening to him.'

One son now has a masters in history, the other studied law and my daughter is a teacher in London. They've all done very well. I'm proud of all three of them. They were great kids for studying, great kids. And we worked hard. We were always there for them at open evenings at school, we were interested in what they were studying and Kathleen was here for them. She gave up nursing to be at home with the children. And now our children are educating their own children to a very high standard.

It was never easy. The work was there, and if you wanted to spend all your life inside in a factory doing overtime, it was there for you. But that wasn't life. We didn't want to do that, and so money wasn't great.

But having the Church, and the social life that went with it, was a great help to us. It provided a structure. I did a lot of shift work, and it was great to be able to go to the Irish clubs and have a laugh and a joke before you had to go back into work, into the serious business of the factory.

We had an allotment and grew all our own stuff – carrots, parsnips, swedes, you name it.

My father had been that type of man also. He had been born in this country. His parents were from a place called Bodyke in Clare. My grandfather had been in the British Army and ended up out in India. My own father worked very hard on the railway to keep nine of us. Hard work killed him eventually. He was self-sufficient, and that rubbed off on us. Pay the rent, he'd say, and the food will look after itself. Keep the four walls around you.

The fact that I had no back door, nothing to go back to, made me take my work seriously. I was ambitious, and no one stood in my way. I started as a barman and ended up as manager of a five-bar business in London. I had to learn how to be assertive when I managed the bars in Marylebone. Sure I knew nothing when I started.

I had two brothers over here before me, but we hadn't much connection with each other. I stood on my own two feet. They were two single men – and died single men. I never thought of them in terms of being there for me if I had problems, although they did encourage Kathleen and me to buy our own home, to make it a base for our children to return to. Having our own home meant that our children had a sense of independence – there was always something to come back to, for them and the grandchildren. It's good to return home to a welcome!

My wife was seventeen when she came to London first; I was twenty. It makes you grow up very quickly.

'I DIDN'T COME OVER AT FIRST WITH
THE INTENTION OF STAYING'

Kathleen Morrissey is a woman in her mid-sixties. She is youthful, elegant and soft-spoken. Her accent has no trace of London, despite fifty years of living in that city. Her speech is pure Galway, with the unmistakable lights and shadows of the native Irish speaker.

Can you tell me something about your original decision to leave Ireland and come to London?

I think the biggest reason was that my mother had died when I was seven. My father was looking after us, but then he got married again two years after her death. I didn't dislike my stepmother; she did her best. But she wasn't my mother.

One of my older brothers, John, had already left to go to London. He thought that there was nothing in Ireland worth staying for, because there were already two brothers on the farm. One of them would inherit the land, so he, John, had to go away in order to have any life for himself. He went and my sister Bridie went with him. Both of them felt it was better to go to England and make their own lives. And once my brother and sister had gone, I felt I wanted to leave, too. It was as though London was where my family was. When I was about fourteen, they wrote and asked me if I'd like to join them for a holiday. And that's how it started.

What part of London had they settled in?

In Kilburn. My uncle Tom Kelly lived in Kilburn and my brother and sister were both staying with him and his family, so, when I came over, I stayed with them also. There were a lot of Irish people in Kilburn and Cricklewood in those days – maybe because it was close to Euston, and close to all the Irish dancehalls. People then used to walk home – they never used taxis or minicabs or whatever. I stayed at my uncle's for a year, and then I rented a room of my own in Kilburn. I was fifteen.

What was it like making your own way in London at fifteen?

It was very, very difficult. We learned to be independent at a very early age. I got the room of my own through a contact of my uncle, a Mr Kennedy, who played in a band in Percy Road. My room was with his family. The rent wasn't a lot, but we never ate much. We kept our money for buying dresses and going dancing.

When I think of my own children, and how things were for them growing up, they were really mollycoddled in comparison. I had to have three jobs to pay my rent. I worked full time in Schweppes, and on Saturdays I worked in Woolworths in Kilburn High Road. I'd another part-time job a few evenings a week in B. B. Evans.

My first day-job was in Schweppes. I was working 'on the belt' as it was called. All the bottles used to go round and round, and we used to have to put labels on them and see that the tops were on correctly. We were working with English girls – they were all English except for myself and my friend Maureen. The others used to be always saying that we weren't doing it right and they used to pick on us a lot. They used to say, 'You Irish, you don't know how to do it properly', or 'What are you doing here?' They'd make some nasty comment or other. That only happened to me in Schweppes, though; I didn't come across it in the other places I worked at that time. And so, we found our own way of getting back at them. As the bottles went around, we'd take one where the top wasn't on right and shake it, hard. Then we'd squirt it all over the English girls, and, of course, we'd get called into the office. We were always getting into trouble over that. Maureen used to get into trouble for name-calling, too – she was great for giving back as good as she got! I'd say a few things back to them, too, but not like Maureen. We all literally worked on top of one another in the factory, so it was at too-close quarters, really. No wonder we fought.

I stayed there in Schweppes for a year, and then I worked in Woolworths, as a permanent job. I liked that; it was very nice. The pay was fairly good there, but they were long hours – nine to six and all day Saturday. Sunday was our only day off. We didn't mind the long hours, though – we used to look forward to going out.

With the three jobs, I earned about ten or twelve pounds a week. That was in 1954 or 1955. I paid five pounds a week rent – that was with having breakfast and my meal cooked for me in the evening. I thought it was good value. I'd spend the rest of my money on a nice dress or a nice skirt – something to go dancing in. I never wore much make-up, just lipstick. I used to go shopping for clothes in the market at Shepherd's Bush. There was fantastic value there.

Tell me about all the dancing you did in those days.

On Fridays and Saturdays we'd go dancing to the Galtymore or the Garryown in Hammersmith, or the Hammersmith Palais. Sometimes we'd go to The Forum in Camden Town. There were a lot of Irish dancehalls here in the fifties. On Sunday afternoons we used to go to the tea-dancing in the Banba club. These were all the ones convenient to home. Occasionally, we'd go to The Round Tower, but you'd have to take the Underground and you'd get home very late. We used to prefer the ones we could walk home from.

I remember dressing up for those nights out. Taffeta was in then – red and black taffeta skirts with gold at the bottom. I'd wear a nice top – maybe white, but something nice, something dressy. We used to do a lot of jiving, so we'd wear flat sandals – the ones with the straps up your legs. We'd get very excited dressing up, and, of course, we'd walk everywhere. We were saving our money, so we couldn't afford to go by bus.

I learned to jive here, when I first came over. I used to go to Percy Road, and they used to have very good dancers there. There was one particular fellow who'd teach us how to jive, and then we went to jiving lessons in Cricklewood Broadway. And we also took ballroom-dancing lessons. Our whole social life revolved around dancing.

I used to go to motorbike racing, too, in Wembley. I'd a friend who liked going, so I went along with her on Thursday nights. We packed a lot into a week. That's when I was working in Woolworths. I don't ever remember being tired – or else the tiredness used to disappear very quickly once we finished work! We used to get paid on a Thursday, and sometimes we wouldn't turn in on a Friday. We were often called into the office over that on a Monday morning. I'd say they guessed what we were up to. We used to say we didn't feel well, or we'd eaten something that disagreed with us, but they knew – I'm sure they did.

You came from an Irish-speaking family, isn't that right?

Yes, we used to speak a fair bit of Irish. When I left home at fourteen, I would have spoken Irish and English more or less equally. That was a huge adjustment for me when I came over here first. I even found the accents very difficult to cope with. When I was working in the shop, they didn't have the tills like they have now. You had to make everything up in your mind, or else write it down. So as I served, I used to add everything up in Irish – we had never done arithmetic through English in school, always in Irish. I never knew how to do it in English. I worked in Woolworths for two years and, to this day, I still do addition and subtraction in my head in Irish – I find I'm quicker at it.

When you left Ireland to come to London, you hadn't even been to Galway! What sort of a first impression did London make on you?

I thought it was absolutely fantastic! Everything was just wonderful! My brother and sister met me and took me shopping to the Edgware Road. There was a big market on Parade Street. Of course, I had no money. My sister Bridie, I remember, bought me a lovely handbag and I was so excited. I thought everywhere was great – I wasn't intimidated in the least. People seemed very nice.

I remember my cousins went to America around the same time that I came to London. I think there were an awful lot of unhappy families left behind in Ireland. I remember Daddy saying to me 'Oh don't go, I'll be so lonely', but I thought I was just going for a holiday, that I'd be back. I really had no idea how I'd feel about London – I didn't come over at first with the intention of staying. I was supposed to go back home after a fortnight, but I wrote to my father and asked him if I could stay. He said, 'Well, if you like it that much, and if your uncle looks after you, then it's okay.' He was really very good to allow me to stay.

I come from a very small place – Killeenaran, close to the village of Ballinderren. There was very little to do there in the fifties – I used to go to a hurling match on Sundays and that was about it. My father was a farmer, so I had no experience whatsoever of city life. London was a complete change for me. But it was so common then – people leaving home to make their lives elsewhere.

My uncle Tom, the one who lived in Kilburn, had been over here for years, and my father knew he'd be very protective of me. My uncle was a plasterer. He worked on the buildings, worked very hard, and he always kept an eye on me. He and his wife, Kathleen, and their two children lived very close by, about ten minutes' walk away. I'd see them on Sundays; I was very well looked after. My older sister, Bridie, was very good to me, too. My younger sister, Margaret, followed me over, and then she stayed with me. That happened a lot in those days – one sister or brother would bring over the other. We're all here now, except for the two brothers, Paddy and Michael, who stayed home to work the farm.

Did you marry young?

I did, yes. I was married at seventeen. I met my husband at the Galtymore. Philip was from Sligo, and he was six years older than me. He had been in London ever since he was seventeen – his parents had emigrated in the late forties and started up a nursing home. I had to get permission to get married, and my father gave me his blessing. I never regretted marrying so young – I was always very happy, very outgoing. I think I was probably quite mature after the two years I'd had looking after myself, managing money, putting a little bit aside for fares or whatever. I learned how to budget, how to be on my own. I missed my family, but I had a brother and sister here.

I remember so many young girls longing to go home: the boat was cheaper then than it is now, but it was still difficult. It was very hard for people who were lonely, who had no solid family here. I think that's why a lot of the fellows who came over used to drink a lot. They probably just had a room, and they didn't want to go back to it on their own, so they just went to the pub. I think that men developed problems with drink *after* they came to London – they most definitely didn't bring those problems with them. They were looking for family, for companionship. They'd have a few drinks and then just go home to bed. The men who worked on the buildings worked very hard, very, very hard. It was a tough life. Men often worked on the lump all their lives, so that at the end of their working life there was nothing for them.

Women tended to join the Church; men went to the pub. I joined the Children of Mary in the church on the Edgware Road. They used to have a meeting on Sunday mornings at eleven. We were quite religious: we used to go to church every Sunday. We used to go to church at home too, but I think it helped a lot more here. There were a lot of different temptations, a lot of ways you could go wrong. If you went to church, it made you feel good for that Sunday, I think. It was a spiritual need you had to fulfil. You'd feel you'd done something good.

My relationship with the Church has remained fairly constant, and I regard it as a very important part of my life. I brought up all my six children as Catholics. It was difficult bringing up a big family, educating and clothing them, but we both liked children, Philip and I. I know that there was the option to control the size of your family, but that wasn't important to us, although it was to some people.

How did you manage to get a home of your own in the first couple of years of your marriage?

It was very difficult to find a place because, wherever you went, nobody wanted the Irish. If the landlord heard you speaking, heard your accent, then the place was suddenly 'gone' – already let. They'd have notices up on boards outside shops and places like that, not in the newspapers, saying, 'No Irish, No Blacks'. We seemed to just accept it, somehow. It was normal. It did bother us a bit, and you knew by the landlord's reaction when you went for an interview for a place that you weren't going to get it. It really wasn't easy.

We had good references from our work, and that eventually stood to us. We got our last flat in Wendover Court, but we had to manage that very carefully.

We went for our interview, and there were these three big nobs waiting for us. A neighbour of mine, Larry Nyland, was working on the road and, just as we came up to him, he lifted his head and said 'Ah, hello Kathleen', and I saw this and said to myself 'Oh, no!' I was afraid, if anyone had seen us, that that would be that.

Anyhow, we went along and did the interview and got the flat. I sat there quietly, while Philip did all the talking. I still had my Galway accent, but his accent was much less recognisably Irish, so I didn't say a word.

We'd had trouble in the early days, too, when we'd two small children. The landlord lived downstairs and we lived upstairs, and naturally the children would be running around. The landlord complained constantly about the noise and kept telling us we should get a place of our own and not be renting with small children. So, anyhow, they gave us notice to leave. We took them to the Tenants' Tribunal – you could take your landlord there if you had a grievance. The Tribunal gave us a stay of a month, but we still had to get out and find somewhere else within that month. I felt very bad at that time – it was an incredible injustice.

Apart from the taunts of the girls in the Schweppes factory, and the difficulties in finding and keeping accommodation, were there other times when you felt uncomfortable, perhaps even isolated, because you were Irish?

Yes, yes I did. During the Troubles, perhaps fifteen or twenty years ago, I found even here that our neighbours' attitude towards us changed. We were out in the garden on one occasion and they said 'You should go back to where you came from.' Another time they said 'You Irish shouldn't be here.' At that stage, we'd lived here for thirty-two years, in this same house. It was very hurtful – they'd been our neighbours for about five or six years. I was really upset over that. I found that when people here were talking about the Troubles, it was best to keep my head down and my mouth shut – it was better to say nothing at all. I didn't find it so much in the workplace, because people there knew me well. But outside, I felt that English people were very much against the Irish. I found a real ignorance about Ireland among people who had never been there – people who would look at you oddly if you were wearing shamrock on St Patrick's Day. I think that racism is still there a bit – not as much as before, but still there.

All the old attitudes around the Irish who used to come to London and work on the buildings and live in one room in Kilburn, they're all changing. The younger Irish people are all very different now. They don't drink as much, and they're very well educated. That's the one that makes the difference. They're into a lot more sport and different hobbies. Long ago, people clung together almost as a matter of survival. They didn't integrate into the community in the way that young Irish people do now.

That's why places like the Galtymore were so important – they weren't just places to dance. They played a very important part in the lives of young Irish people in the fifties – and I think they do still. You can go and meet people there and it's a really good night out; people really talk to one another. I believe it's like a community meeting-point – people of all ages from seventeen to seventy meet up in the Galtymore, and that has always been the way. I'm really sad that the Galtymore is the only one of the Irish dancehalls left – and everyone who goes there says the same thing. It's been open since the early fifties, and it's still going strong, and I hope that it continues. It was the one place you'd always meet a friendly face. I'd say quite a bit of business was transacted there, too. In the early days, if we needed a plumber or an electrician we'd always find one at the Galty! It was a great big network, really. For me, in so many ways, it was the most significant place in my life in London.

I still go there – three nights a week – Friday, Saturday and Sunday. I think it's even better now because, when we used to go years ago, the men used to be very shy. They wouldn't ask the girls to dance. But now, they don't seem to be so shy. At one time, the

Galtymore was just one big ballroom, but now it's divided in two. One part is for the younger people and the other for the more middle-aged. But both sides still mix. You don't see any of the fighting we used to see when we were younger. It would happen very seldom these days. I think that most of those fights were over girls! Men would come in once the pubs had closed, and the amount of drink on them had a lot to do with it. They still come in late, but they don't fight. The bouncers protect them from one another – if there are any signs of trouble, they move in immediately.

You left school before your Inter Cert. Did you ever have any inclination to return to school?

Not at first. I was more interested in getting out to work. But then, after a while, I had a friend who decided we'd go and study at night. We used to go twice a week, and we did quite a lot of different night-classes. First of all, we went in for nursing, and we did that for a year part time. I think that was on a Tuesday night. We led very full lives! Dancing on Friday, Saturday and Sunday; motorbike racing on Thursday; and night-classes on Tuesday.

After that year, I went and worked for my mother-in-law in her nursing-home for two years, and I just continued nursing after that. At the moment, I look after a disabled girl with cerebral palsy. It's intensive nursing – one-to-one care – but I enjoy it. I'll keep doing this work as long as I can.

How would you feel about going back to Ireland?

A lot of people of my age have gone back. I've got my own cottage there, in Killeenaran. It has a thatched roof, and I've extended out the back and added another floor. It used to be just the ground floor, with three rooms. It's the old house, the one I was born in, and I have a huge emotional attachment to it. Seven of us, including my parents, used to live in those three rooms. I have only a few memories of my mother and her last illness. I remember crying as she was taken away from the cottage. She told me not to; she tried to comfort me, telling me she'd be back tomorrow. But she never came back.

The old house used to be very cramped. Now it has a dining-room, bathroom and toilet as well. At the side, what was a shed, there is now a room which will become a games room. I'm very proud of it.

I don't know if I'd ever go back to live there permanently – I might do, one day. I think it would take a few years to settle back. But there is a dancehall in Oranmore! We go there every time I go home. It's not as mixed as the Galtymore – more the one age group. It brings lots of people, particularly when the Galway races are on.

But really, I'm very settled now. I've a son and a daughter living near me here in London. Everything is very convenient here; I find when I go home, because I live in the country, it takes a long time to get into town and the day is gone. I know it's not as bad as it used to be, but here there are so many different things close together. Even though I was born and bred in the country, I think I'm a city person now.

Although I'm well settled here, I feel much more at home when I'm in Ireland. Definitely. I love it here and everything is fantastic, but when I'm going to Ireland I still say 'I'm going home.' When I'm coming back to London, I say 'I'm going back to England.' Ireland is where my heart is.

I go and stay in my cottage maybe three or four times a year. Ireland has changed a lot for the better over the years. The shopping facilities are so much better, everything is more convenient, but you still need a car. And the euro has brought big changes, too. I think the quality of people's lives is better – their homes and what they have in their homes. Even better than here!

When I stay in my cottage, I have the sense that nothing has changed, that nothing is missing. I still have all my memories there. My children come too, and they love it. My younger son is very much for Ireland, and my daughter who lives there, she is too, of course. My other four daughters are quite happy to be half-Irish and half-English. They love Ireland. When they were small, they used to go back for eight weeks each summer, back to the farm. They have the best of both worlds, and they go back and forwards a lot. And my grandchildren are all aware of their Irish roots, too. My daughters keep them up with Ireland.

We tried moving back to Ireland when our own children were small, but it didn't work out. What happened was, my husband went out to Canada to look for work in 1956. I went back to Ireland, to my family home, with my nine-month-old daughter, Catherine. It was wonderful: my brothers, Paddy and Michael, and my father and stepmother were so good to us. I loved being home; I even won a beauty contest in the Hangar Club in Galway – I was Queen of the Céilí! I won a silver cup, a crown and twenty-five pounds! I was so excited, and everybody was very proud, particularly Daddy. I didn't care about the money, I was just so thrilled to have won! My sister Bridie had won it the year before, so there were great celebrations. Daddy was delighted with the money, too – in those days, twenty-five pounds made a difference.

I stayed with them all in Killeenaran for a year and then joined Philip in Canada. My daughter, Patricia, was born in Toronto the following year. We stayed in Canada for three years, but I wasn't happy. I just couldn't settle. I really wanted to go back to Ireland. So we went to Dublin and lived in Rathfarnham for two years, from 1962–1964. We had four children at that time. The older two were very excited about going. They thought it was great. They went to school in Terenure. That was difficult for them, though – they were supposed to speak Irish, but they just couldn't catch up. They didn't like that.

I found it difficult being back, too, even though people were very friendly. I found it a big change not to go out to work. In the early sixties in Dublin, mothers did not go out to work, and that was a difficult adjustment for me. We had decided to live in my mother-in-law's house in Rathfarnham until we saw how things went, so at least we had no rent to pay. But my husband couldn't get work – times were pretty lean in Dublin then. We stuck it out for two years, until we knew it wasn't going to work. We were very disappointed that it hadn't. My brothers used to come up and visit, and my father. That was nice. But it didn't work out, and we got very disheartened.

I think the point in your life for going home passes – if it doesn't work the first time, it's not possible to try again. We never did. We made the decision that London was our home. It would have been too heartbreaking to go through that again.

Does your life still gravitate towards the Irish community now, or do you have English friends as well?

No. All Irish. All my friends are Irish. I suppose I haven't really assimilated, but I have no regrets about that. I do mix with other nationalities at work, but my friends are Irish. I sometimes visit my sisters on a Sunday, and I go out quite a bit with my friend, Carmel. She saves a seat for me in the Galtymore at the weekends. I go out with my boyfriend on Saturday and Sunday – I met him two years ago at the Galtymore.

Philip died ten years ago, and it changed my life completely. I had nobody to talk to, nobody to discuss things with. I didn't go out for five years after his death. I mean, I visited my sister and did family things like that, but I never went out socially. Then my daughter insisted I went dancing. So I went back to the Galtymore. And it was the Galtymore that really helped me pick up the pieces. The first time, I thought, no, I can't do this, but after two or three times I was the one who said to my daughter 'Come on, let's go dancing!'

I met a man from Limerick some time ago, and I went out with him for three and a half years. Then he wanted a break for four months. I found that very hard to take, and it was unexpected. He was too used to being a bachelor. But I'm very happy now: I'm with a man from Donegal – I've never had an English boyfriend!

You're here fifty years. Do you have any regrets?

No, none. None at all. I've had six children, I have my own modernised cottage in Ireland and I have everything I want. I think I've done better financially here than if I'd stayed in Ireland.

But things are changing in London, too. I'm glad that my children are reared – drugs are a real fear now. And you can't walk out in the evenings anymore, the way we used to walk home from the dancehalls. I'd be much more nervous about my personal safety these days: even driving, you have to be careful and keep your doors locked.

I love where I live in Edgware, the people are very nice and everything is very central. I know a lot of people from the Church, too. But living here, you can get on with things without everyone knowing your business. The downside of that is when something goes wrong you don't get help as easily. For instance, when my husband died the local priest never even came to see me. The priests are not as close to the people. Having said that, an Irish priest, Fr Tom Kiernan, was wonderful to me around that time. He used to stay with Philip in the hospital all day, and he'd always make sure that I was all right. I've never forgotten his kindness. But it must have been very difficult for people who had no family here when things went wrong.

I don't think I'd have been able to have the sort of career I now have if I'd stayed at home in Ireland. There were more opportunities here.

I've no regrets, none at all.

'KILBURN AND CRICKLEWOOD WERE BURSTING AT THE SEAMS WITH IRISH'

Mary Walker (not her real name) is a vibrant, energetic woman, who looks considerably younger than her sixty-six years. She returned to live in Ireland in August 2000, after four decades of life in North London. She has chosen to remain anonymous, lest any of her reminiscences be hurtful to others. To respect that wish for anonymity, all the names of people mentioned during our interview have been changed.

You left Ireland for London in September 1959. Can you tell me why you made the decision to leave?

I was working in Dublin as a hairdresser at that time. After I'd worked in two different salons, one on the quays and another in Thomas Street, whose name I'm still trying to remember, I decided I wanted something different. I went to London for a year's experience, which somehow ended up being forty-one years of experience.

I was twenty-three then – not nearly as young as some of the other girls who went to London around that time. But London wasn't my first move. I was born in Tyrone, and we'd had to move to Dublin because my father lost his business there. We came south because he had to get a job. After all, he had all these children to look after – there were eight of us and I was the eldest. It's something I don't like to talk about – surprisingly enough, it's still very painful after all these years. I had this good life, and then it was taken away from me. I felt that I had been uprooted at fifteen.

But I'd always been pretty determined, and I decided I wanted to be a hairdresser. In those days, in the fifties, that wasn't seen as a good choice. It was met with 'What do you want to do that for?' It was a struggle, a big struggle. My parents did support me, even though they didn't like the idea at first. You had to pay a fee in those days. For the first year, I got no money at all – we were really dogsbodies. It was pure exploitation. We washed the towels, polished the floor, whatever was needed. I had to train for three years, and then I was what was called an 'improver'. Those were the days when salons were making big money – the 'teddy boy' and 'teddy girl' days. The teddy girls all had poodle cuts then, and there was a great turnover of business because they had a perm every six weeks.

I suppose it wasn't real economic need which drove me, as I already had a job, but more a need for adventure. I went over with a friend, whose sister from Dublin was already there. We stayed with her for a while and then I got a bedsit of my own. By then I was anxious to adapt to living alone – I was already away, far from home, and I wanted to be independent.

Can you remember your first job?

My first job was working for a Frenchman in his hairdressing salon in Hampstead. I took the job immediately it was offered. I'd gone over with just a week's wages, and I had to pay the rent. That's how it was in those days: you didn't have a credit card or anything like that. You took the first job, just to have a job. You grew up very quickly like that.

This Frenchman more or less 'polished me up', I might say. He was very charming. He was short and dumpy, and he insisted on calling me 'Maria'. I'd say 'No, my name is Mary.' The salon was very plush, and he had this glamorous-looking wife. She was a lot younger than him, always very well made-up, with her two sets of false eyelashes. I'd arrive in the mornings, already with my make-up on, and he'd always send me off telling me to put on some more because I was working under lights. Everything was 'Madame' – 'Take Madame's coat' – and so on. He was a very good hairdresser; working for him was excellent training. Chez Raymond, I remember, was the name of the salon. A posh place. He taught me a lot of new hairdressing techniques – it was a big change from Dublin and the girls with their poodle cuts! And the duck's arse! Working with him gave me a lot more confidence. He taught me how to make Greek coffee, too. Both he and his wife were very nice to me. I stayed with him almost twelve months.

Then I went for this job in Cricklewood, in a salon run by Greeks. One of the other men working at Raymond's had said to me that I'd need to get myself out of there, that I wasn't mixing with any of my own kind. Otherwise, I'd get stuck in that kind of Hampstead ambience. He knew this Greek man who had two salons in Cricklewood, so I went along for an interview. I got the job. I think I wanted it for two reasons – one, because it offered more money, and two, because I wanted to mix with more ordinary people, Irish people, working-class people.

There were an awful lot of Irish coming to the salon in Cricklewood. It was a big place – there were nine of us, nine assistants. I was there for nearly nine years. It wasn't usual in those days to see an Irish girl as a hairdresser. Lots of other nationalities went into hairdressing, but not the Irish. The Greeks and the Italians were predominant in the business. Irish girls tended to work in the big factories, and the men worked on the buildings – at least, that's what I saw. I was fortunate that I went with a skill – more so than an education. So many people arrived without any skills at all.

Did you find it difficult to get accommodation in those early days?

It wasn't easy – the London of 1959 was not the London of today. Those were the times when the Irish had to look in the phone box for accommodation details – that's where the rooms to let were advertised. Nowadays, it's all 'models' and the rest of it that advertise in the phone kiosks, but back then, that's how you found your room. And it's true what they say – in those days it was 'no dogs, blacks or Irish', or maybe even 'no Irish, blacks or dogs'. The ads in the kiosk would give you a phone number, and maybe the name of the road, and that was all. You had to phone for directions after that, and it was difficult – the Irish didn't have a very good name then, as they were classed as dirty.

The first flat I had on my own was in Kensal Rise, North London. I didn't stay there long – the landlady had a thing about the Irish. She'd had Irish girls before, nurses mostly, and she said that they were dirty. She had that kind of attitude – 'Oh, well, even though you're Irish, I'll let you have it anyway – you look all right.' I was disgusted by that, and I said to myself 'I'll show you, then.' When I left, and told the landlady she could have her room, I polished the lino so much you'd almost break your neck on it.

Of all the other things in my life, I still remember that landlady's face and the room she rented to me. There was a bathroom which we all shared, and she had notes everywhere: 'Don't drop talcum powder on the floor' – don't do this, don't do that. It was an old house in Kensal Rise, three storeys, with only a twenty-watt bulb for those high ceilings. Of course, you couldn't have anybody to stay, let alone do anything wrong. You couldn't even have anyone in for coffee. At eleven o'clock at night, the landlady's husband would be standing at the top of the stairs in his pyjamas, making sure every visitor was out.

When I was working and living in Hampstead, I didn't get to know any Irish at all. Most of the clients in the salon were very manicured ladies, so I wasn't really mixing. One client of mine, a Scottish girl who became a good friend, said to me 'Mary, you'd want to move along.' There was a room going in the house where she lived, and she encouraged me to go for it. So I moved to a place just off Kilburn. Remember that these were all bedsits in houses where the landlords and landladies still lived. The room there was so sparse that I can still remember it to this day. There was a browny-green lino on the floor and the same covering on the table. There were grey blankets on the bed and a cupboard in the corner which was a wardrobe. That was about it. I still have nightmares about that room. That's what they were like in those days. The landlords didn't care. The room backed onto the railway, so all the windows used to rattle. The kids today don't know what I'm talking about, but there was a gas ring that used to come out of the wall and it sat on the table. That was your 'cooking facilities'. I cooked whatever would fit into one pan, or one pot. It was all a bit of a shock to the system. In Dublin, I'd shared a flat in Rathmines with another girl and we had a lovely – well, in those days it was lovely – bedroom, a sitting-room and a kitchen on the landing. It was a three-storey house, on a real student street, a great fun place to be. Then I left all that for this palace in Kilburn. I paid one pound ten shillings a week in rent. I wasn't the only one living like that – that's the way it was.

Mind you, the Irish themselves became landlords too, when they moved up. Some of them even learned to speak with a plum in their mouths. That used to amaze me: they'd only made money, not changed class. Irish clients of mine did it: they'd buy a house and live in one room themselves, and rent out all the others. That's where a lot of the Irish made money. There were all these men working on the buildings and earning great money. They worked seven days a week, those men, and when they got married, they bought a house like that. Those women clients of mine became very wealthy, and their husbands ended up as contractors and subbies. I should have married one like that!

At that time, I was bringing home about six pounds a week, which was good money. I was working all the hours God sent but, being a hairdresser, I also got a few tips.

By this stage, you were over a year in London, with no plans to go home. What appealed to you about London enough to make you stay?

I don't know that there was a lot that appealed to me about it in those days – I suppose it was more about surviving, really, about living. It wasn't that I said 'This is what I'm going to do now' – in those days, if you had a job which paid well, paid the rent, it meant you were able to go places. Staying on just happened. After the first year, I had no really strong yearnings to come back to Ireland. I don't remember even thinking 'What would I be going back to?' Staying here became a habit, and a lot of that was to do with having a good job. And I got in with a crowd of girls in Cricklewood and made friends. I felt more at home there than I had in Hampstead. There was a big Irish clientele in the salon, as well as a big Jewish clientele. The days were divided like that, too – the Jewish ladies in the mornings, the Irish ladies before the kids came out of school and then the factory girls in the late afternoon.

What sort of memories do you have of Cricklewood forty years ago?

Kilburn and Cricklewood at that time were bursting at the seams with Irish. There were a lot of factories around Cricklewood in those days. There was a big Smyth's that made clocks and speedometers, things like that. Another factory manufactured washing machines, Rose Razor, and then there was Frigidaire. They were all around Collindale, all that area. It felt like the whole of London came out of Smith's on a Friday afternoon. You couldn't walk along the footpaths at a quarter past four, when the factories finished. And there was Schweppes – so there were a lot of big factories in the area then that aren't there anymore. A lot of Irish girls worked in those factories. As a result, in the salon we didn't finish work until nine o'clock at night. The girls would come from the factories at around half four, five o'clock, so we had to start the day's work then.

In Cricklewood, I lived over one of the salons. I remember the

Paddy-wagons, as they called them, coming around at night after the Galtymore. All I can say is, the police had an easy time of it. All they'd do is pick up the poor fellows who were drunk and throw them into the back of the wagons. Harmless poor fellows – they were just a bit wobbly. No knives, no guns, no drugs. No aggression at all. It was a piece of cake. The police just piled them in like lumps of meat and off they went. There were often fights, too, and most of them were over women, or football. For all the years I lived in Cricklewood, I never once went to the Galtymore.

Our social lives revolved around dancing, though. I loved the Hammersmith Palais, which was a long way away. Joe Loss was my favourite: if I didn't get a fix of Joe Loss on a weekly basis, I'd be in very bad form. Because of the long hours I worked, I really didn't have time for any sort of social life, other than dancing. I don't think I could have afforded anything else, anyway. I used to read a lot, too. I'd buy books, or clients would give them to me. With your rent, travel, food, bits of clothes, make-up, it didn't take long to eat up your wages.

You had to feed the meter in your room, too, and that cost a lot of money. The landlords had them regulated – you might put a shilling in and only get a few pence worth of electricity out of it. The landlords and landladies emptied the meters themselves; they made a fortune out of them. They conned you every way.

I remember one night after we'd been to Hammersmith, none of us had any money left to get home. We walked from Hammersmith to Kilburn – away over the other side of London, across the bridge, over the water. One New Year's Eve we finished work too late to go to Hammersmith. One of the girls said we'd have to queue for too long, and then we'd probably not get in, and we'd never get transport home, so we went to a local ballroom in Kilburn, the State – it didn't last for long, that one; I think it was only open for a couple of years. But it was enough for me to meet my Waterloo. That was the night I met my husband. He was from

Poland, an engineer. We were happy at the beginning, but I think I attract the ones who are looking for a cosy life.

Did life change for you in many ways once you'd married?

I was twenty-six when I got married. I don't even know that I wanted to. I think it's great today, where people can live together until they get to know one another. There's more options. We were turfed into marriage, and suddenly you had a man to look after, to cook all these dinners that he expected to be like his mother's. Anyway, a couple of years after we got married, I went for an interview with the Halifax, in their Head Office. I didn't tell my husband I was going for the interview, because I kind of knew what his reaction would be. I was right. I got the job, and my husband really resented this, told me I wasn't able for it – and I think things started going downhill from there. He thought I was getting too big for my boots. All I could think of was that I'd now be getting Saturdays off, and I'd qualify for a staff mortgage and all the perks. We were able to buy a house in Edgware. But it all had a bad effect on him – he thought I was getting too far ahead of him. It was hard to understand – I was doing this for both of us; he was benefiting, too. But he didn't seem to see it like that.

It was a very stressful job at the Halifax, but I just did it. At the time I didn't think I was being brave. I worked long hours and over the years built up more and more clients, which meant I had more and more work. I was coming home exhausted. I remember being fed up, but it was a case of getting on with it, surviving. I'd have liked a family, but my husband didn't seem to think about that. We were married for fifteen years. During all that time, our friends were mostly eastern Europeans, men married to English girls for the most part. There was a big group of us – nearly all divorced now, not just me.

We were back and forwards to Poland a lot – he'd tell me when we were going. And I was the one who had to do all the saving for those holidays. In many ways, the culture in Poland was similar to ours – they were religious people; his aunts all went to church and did the First Fridays, all that sort of thing. The upbringing would have been very similar. Just a different language, different food, but the ideas, the culture – they were all very like our own.

The sense of humour was different though. I remember I'd say something, slagging somebody – even myself – and my husband would say 'What do you mean?' I gave up. 'Oh, talk to yourself, Mary,' I'd say.

Did you have any contact with Ireland during those years?

I remember we came to Ireland after we got married, and then I wasn't home again for a very long time. I think – in fact I know – that I lost a lot of my identity during those years. After I got divorced, I went back to the salon in Cricklewood for one morning a week. I was still working at the Halifax, bringing home overtime as well. I had to – I had to pay my husband off. And after I took early retirement from the Halifax, I started hairdressing again from home.

I had a lovely lodger, a Chinese man, and he said to me that I should do something other than hairdressing from home – something to get out a bit more. So, I went to St Anthony's in Edgware – there's the church and the club there, both predominantly Irish – and one day I just asked Fr Kiernan, flippant like, 'Would you have a job for me, Father?' And he said 'There's a job going down in the bar – would you do that?' And I said 'I'd do anything, Father.' So I went and worked there part time, and that was an education!

The Irish club was a very busy place – it was a real lease of life for me. It's very quiet these days, but twelve years ago or so, three of us would be kept going on a Sunday night. I got my own identity back, working there with the Irish. My sense of humour returned.

Most of the people I came across were from Mayo, Cork and Kerry. Not too many from my end of the world, and not many from the midlands either. I used to think that there was nobody left in Mayo – they're all in London! Great group, great spenders, all of them. I'd meet people in the Irish club that I'd never meet in my ordinary life. Working behind the bar I met so many lovely people, lovely men. They knew how to joke and to take it to a certain point – I'd cut it off if it started going, well … And they all knew that. Oh, they'd eff and blind from time to time, but just the normal stuff.

They were a great group in the club. That's how the clubs started out – they were a place in a big city where the Irish could feel at home. They'd have their own associations and association dinner dances, that kind of thing. The club used to have a big room, and that was their community, where they all used to meet. The fellows who worked on the buildings would all meet each other there, and it was part club, part business, part family meeting-place. They'd bring the kids, and the kids would grow up around going to church and the club, and then bring their own kids.

The clubs were mostly attached to churches, and some of them were very big. The biggest Irish club that I can remember was Quex Road in Kilburn. And by the way, Bishop Eamon Casey did an awful lot of good for people in Quex Road. People with housing problems particularly. He was a very good man in that way.

They held an awful lot of social events in Quex Road. But like everything else now, the Irish are very spread out. In those days, they stayed with their own. And that's all dying out, now.

What sort of role do you think the Catholic Church played in the lives of the Irish?

Well, I observed that quite a bit, both personally speaking and watching others. It all depends on the priest, doesn't it? Fr Kiernan in Edgware was wonderful – everything was very quietly done for those who needed help. If there was somebody who died in

London, somebody who couldn't afford to come home, he came up with the goods. He's retired now and living in Dublin. I knew a lot about the people he helped – I lived in Edgware for thirty-six years. If somebody had a tragedy and couldn't afford the funeral, he'd step in, and we'd provide the food. He was marvellous, from a practical as well as a spiritual point of view. I couldn't say a word against him. I've heard so many stories from the women he helped.

I've had many a heated discussion with people giving out about the Church. A lot of the Irish don't want to get involved, but they like to grumble about what somebody's not doing. So many people I've come across would say 'Why doesn't he do this? Why doesn't he do that?' Not that they'd be prepared to roll up their sleeves themselves. I used to turn around to them and say 'Why don't you put it to Father Kiernan? Why don't you ask him?' They wouldn't be prepared to talk to him, talk as a man, say to him that such a thing needed doing. He'd often ask me 'What was my sermon like?' and I'd say 'Oh, Father, it was too long!' He'd ask you for feedback, and he'd really want it. He never talked about the people he helped, so others didn't know. I think I had a fairly good insight into all that.

When people were in London in the early days, there was a lot of activity around the Church. You got to know a lot of people by going to church. I don't think the practice of religion fell off in those days – we were more or less brainwashed. I did fall a bit myself – it didn't disturb me if I didn't go to Mass. I didn't give up, but I didn't have a conscience about it. It was often very funny listening to people worrying about contraception, but my decisions were private ones.

Have attitudes towards the Irish changed over the years?

Long ago, the Irish had the reputation of being big drinkers and fighters. That's all changed now. But in those days, young men coming from big families were suddenly thrust into one room, and they couldn't cope with the loneliness. Most of those young fellows didn't have a drink problem when they came to London first – they developed it afterwards, looking for company in the pub. They had landladies who didn't want them in their room – where else could they go? I saw them, poor young fellows. On Saturdays, they'd go to a restaurant for lunch. Then the poor fellows went off to the launderette next door, and then they'd come back and it was off to the pub. The landladies didn't want them in the house. Some who were in lodgings got an evening meal, but others just rented a room. Like myself – the room with the gas ring that you pulled out of the wall.

I often saw those poor young fellows at the post office on Saturday mornings, sending home the postal order with most of their wages. It was like a religion. It would break your heart. Those are some of the men that the Aisling project is trying to repatriate now. And it's right: they're some of the men that kept the rural economy going in Ireland for years.

And there were the huge numbers of young girls who went into service. Edgware was full of Irish girls living in Jewish homes. At least they were quite well off – they got fed, they had a roof over their heads and they'd no travelling expenses. But they were so innocent, so young, some of them no more than fifteen or sixteen, out from the West of Ireland. It's a miracle more of them didn't get into trouble. Still, we had the best contraception of all – fear!

If one of them did get pregnant, that poor girl would have to live in one room. Or else she got married to the fellow, and then the three of them would live in the room. That was the norm in Cricklewood. And don't forget there was no social. Those young girls had to keep working, no matter what. And going home to Ireland was not an option. A lot of them, their kids were going to school before anyone in Ireland knew that they existed. It was terrible, really. Those girls really suffered, and the men got away with it.

Irish girls worked a lot in shops, too – places like Boots and John Lewis – and in all the pubs and restaurants. My sisters worked all their lives in department stores – they came over and stayed with me after I got married.

And don't forget that London was a very bleak place in the fifties. It was just after the War, and little bits of sunshine were only beginning to break through when I went there first. It was a very local kind of living, like a series of villages – your bread shop, your butcher's shop, none of the big supermarkets. And that's why London never struck me as vast or intimidating. I lived in a village – size never struck me unless I went up the West End. A lot of people owned their own shops around Cricklewood – the grocer was Italian, the fish man was Greek. They were doing well because they owned their own businesses.

Things are very different these days, but long ago there was the perception of the Irish as 'thick'. Cockney people used to have that attitude towards the Irish. They saw themselves as superior. But then, they'd lived in the East End of London all their lives, in terrible poverty, so they didn't know any better either. A lot of English people had the idea that the Irish still lived in hovels. Some of the Irish brought it on themselves – those who had no education coming over here. It's ignorance, of course, on the part of English people, too, who then stereotype us.

I found that superior attitude with clients, too, often Jewish clients. Many of them were very good to me, but they did want their pound of flesh. When they said 'jump', you jumped. I was still in the hairdressing for a couple of years after I got married, before I took the job with the Halifax. All the weddings and bar mitzvahs took place on Sundays, when there were no salons open. So I'd have to go to their homes. They'd send a car for me. If they were very rich and very nice, I was just called 'Mary'. Otherwise, I was 'the hairdresser'. It didn't matter to me. But it was hard going, working on Sundays. I might have been out on the Saturday night, and my husband would be shouting at me for going out to work on Sundays, saying to me 'Why don't you go and live with those Jews?' He didn't mind the money, though. I earned good money for Sundays.

But, you know, the prejudice that the Irish used to suffer they now feel about Pakistanis – they don't want them in their area. Edgware used to be a predominantly Jewish area – you got dressed up to go to Edgware. Now it's all fast food, and predominantly Irish with Pakistanis and Indians. Once the Irish got money, they moved out of Cricklewood, to nicer areas like Edgware and Stanmore. And now the Pakistanis are moving out, doing the same thing.

What sort of cultural differences did you notice between life in London and the Ireland of 2000?

I'd started to come back to Ireland again in the eighties, after a long gap. The first thing I noticed was the prosperity, even then – the difference from when I'd left. It was a slow difference, but a visual difference. By the end of the nineties, all the houses had extensions on – there were a lot of big improvements. I noticed all the high-powered salons in Dublin. And everybody had a choice of jobs. Before, you got a job and, whether you liked it or not, you stayed. I found that that was great – that range of choice. And to see women back at work part time – I thought that that was great, too, especially for married women. It used to be that you got married, and that was it.

I think, though, there's a huge tendency in Ireland to be critical of others, even for petty things, things that I would tend to ignore. Perhaps it's me that has changed: I've lived for over forty years in the hubbub of a fast-moving city, where you didn't know others in the sense that you do here. I knew my neighbours, in that I knew who they were, but I didn't know them in any real sense.

Since I've come home to Ireland to stay, I've begun to wonder are the Irish really as sincere as they come across, or are they just being nosey. I didn't understand that in the beginning, because I wasn't used to the intrusiveness. I don't think I even noticed the anonymity of London while I was living there – it just became my way of life over the forty-one years I spent there. I came out the door in the mornings, probably with a piece of toast in my hand, down the road to the Underground, all the way into town on a packed train: nobody took any notice of others around them. You came back the same way. I couldn't tell you who I saw in the course of those journeys. You didn't speak or acknowledge other people: that was just the culture.

I worked with all nationalities, and I found that interesting. It was nice to have friends from different backgrounds – and I still have them. Chinese, Maltese – all very sincere people. I think that living in London was good for my personal development. I think it's good for everybody to have lived away. A nephew of mine said that recently. He said that if everybody was shipped away for a couple of years, they'd come back having lost a lot of the rubbish that they talk. He feels that people who have lived away are more open to difference.

When I decided to buy my flat here, the reaction was great. 'No problem, Mary,' I was told, and 'Yeah, you're grand.' But it wasn't grand, and I found that people did not do as they'd promised. For example, I had no stamp duty to pay, according to the brochure. So, the sale was going ahead, and I was trying to manage the purchase from London. My London solicitor was on the ball, but the only response we could get from here was that everything was 'grand'. Just before I moved, I got a bill in the post from my solicitor in Ireland, and included was four thousand pounds for stamp duty. And my Irish solicitor had gone off on his holidays! I was tearing my hair out all over that weekend. People hadn't done their homework here – it was very stressful.

Here, in Ireland, I feel you are more restricted in what you can say. You're worried how it's going to be analysed, so you've got to be more careful. I've had the experience of saying something that I meant in general, and having people pick holes in it as though I meant it in particular, that I was being personal. And I wasn't. I was simply making a general observation.

Do you have the distinction in your mind between 'heart home' and 'made home'?

I think everybody has that. No matter how long you've been away, you're still Irish, there's still something about you. When I go to Tyrone, for example, I still feel that I belong there. I left there a very long time ago, and it's hard to explain – but that's where my roots are. I have an affinity – or whatever word you'd care to use – with the place. I still feel that way. I met very few Northern Irish people in London – the vast majority of the people I knew were from the south and the west of the country.

When the Troubles happened, I used to get a lot of sly remarks when I worked in the Halifax. It made me very uncomfortable, and very angry at times. 'Why don't they just pull the plug and let it go down?' Nothing was ever said face to face to me – just loud enough so that I could hear it. I was meant to hear it. I'd know people were talking about it, even though not to me directly. They'd say 'Oh, Ireland's a terrible place.' Some of those people were so ignorant they didn't even know that Ireland was divided, with the Six Counties under British rule. But it was pointless getting into an argument with those people. They knew nothing about King Billy: there were a lot of southern Irish that I met who knew nothing about King Billy, but I grew up with him. I know what he looks like on a big flag.

But you knew the areas to avoid – like you do in any big city. You go out in the country areas in Northern Ireland, and everybody's drinking in the same pub. It's not as bad as people think it is. In Omagh, Protestant and Catholic alike attended each other's funerals. Everybody had suffered. And I had personal experience of that myself – I knew people who died in the Omagh bombing, relatives of my nephew's wife.

When bombs went off in Harrods and places like that – they were very uncomfortable times. You did feel like not saying very much. But then you knew the people who were doing it were crazy, and some English people understood that it was just the terrorists who were doing those things. At the same time, there was a lot of anger, an awful lot of anger.

I still don't think that English people quite understand the Peace Process. I truly believe they don't understand how things go so deep. We can hardly understand it ourselves. With the media coverage there is in England, people think it's just Protestant against Catholic. It's a handy shorthand – that's it to them. It's all very difficult.

When I was going to school, there was the Catholic school on the one side, and the Protestant on the other. 'Proddy bitch' and 'papist bitch' were the words we used at one another – we didn't know why! As kids we threw insults at each other – having the schools opposite was like a red rag to a bull – but we didn't know why.

And now so much of it is about drugs money. People fighting with each other who've never been inside a church.

You worked in St Anthony's Irish club for some years and got to know a lot of other Irish people of your generation. What was their vision of coming home after such a long time in London?

I think a lot of them fantasised about owning the little bit of land down the country. A lot of them didn't see further than that. Even after decades in London, they talked as though they still lived here, down the country. God knows how long they'd lived in Edgware, but they hadn't moved on in so many ways. They'd have a good old go at England and at Lizzie, the Queen, often to annoy me, really. They'd arrived in London at starvation level, often with no shoes on their feet, and made a good living, but still talked about Ireland as 'Ah, it's a great country.'

There are so many Irish people in England who didn't want to be there. They had to go, for the work. Even though they'd physically gone over on the boat, they still lived in Ireland, in this dream-world of how wonderful it was. And it wasn't wonderful. Sometimes you'd get a little bit of honesty, when people were prepared to be realistic and say 'Yes, we did earn a good living' or 'England has been good to us' – and it was good to me, too. Otherwise you wouldn't live in it.

A lot of them have fantasies about going back home. But when are they going back? They don't want to give up the money they're earning, the life they have in London and all the good things that go with it. They're physically working away, but their minds are here. I've often said to them 'Why don't you go back and try it?' And they'd say 'Oh, but it's very expensive in Ireland.' But they say this without doing any research, or making a bit of a plan. It's expensive in London, too.

But they'd rather just talk about it. The old days. You'd swear listening to them that you were sitting in Ireland forty years ago, rather than in St Anthony's club in Edgware.

What were your own hopes and dreams about coming home?

Deep down inside, I always had the feeling that I would like to settle here in Ireland. It wasn't always prominent, but it was bubbling away over the last couple of years. I knew I couldn't keep going as I was. I had a house to keep – I was on my own – I was working at two jobs and doing bits and pieces everywhere to keep the house in decent order. I felt as though I was juggling everything, and I was getting tired. I could feel it coming along – bit by bit, I could feel that I wasn't able to do what I'd been doing six months before. And that was foremost in my mind – I knew I couldn't do this for the rest of my life. It was too much of a struggle to keep my house in London just standing – and I'm on my own, I have no children. I knew I had to make a decision, and the pull was really to come back to Ireland.

And then when I saw this apartment, everything just fell into place. I was ready. Although I hadn't put a time on my decision, the decision was already made. I saw this place in May, and by the end of July I was here, moved in with boxes and all. Once I saw this door, I got a feeling that it was right. My house in Edgware sold at once, with no problems. Well, we'd a bit of haggling to do, but I held out and I got almost what I was looking for. The strangest thing was that the buyers only came once – they never even came back to check anything! So it was all done very quickly. It was like it was meant to be. It all seems uncanny now.

When I told friends back in London, they were gobsmacked. Some people tried to discourage me, but I just shut those out. I knew the kind of people I was dealing with. Other people talked about how brave I was. I said I wasn't brave at all – it just hadn't hit home yet! When they talked about the expense, I reminded them of Council tax in England, water rates, parking taxes where I lived. I haven't got any of that now. They couldn't believe it – 'What, no Council tax, no water rates?' The Council tax is over twelve hundred pounds a year – that's an awful lot of money. From a financial point of view, I'm better off here.

The first few months after I came back were very tiring. I was exhausted all the time, so I didn't have time to think. I had to find a doctor, make a will, sort out all the bureaucracy – there were lots of things to do. I discovered afterwards that I had a health problem which should have been spotted in London, and the care I've got from St James's hospital is wonderful. I've been very lucky, moving to Newbridge. The hospital have really looked after me, changed my medication, sorted out my tiredness. And I have a great GP – a lot of good things have come out of this move. From a health point of view, it was a bit scary, but I feel very fortunate now.

I'm home just over two years, and in the last six months things have begun to feel more real. I'm feeling a lot better; things are more normal. I have a real sense that this is now home. Last week,

I really realised it. I'd been away for two weeks, and I thought 'I'm ready to go home.'

My old neighbours in Edgware asked me 'What do you think about your old home across the street?' It was just a house – I felt no connection to it. I can't believe it myself that I lived in that house for over thirty-six years and I didn't feel a thing. I was waiting for a reaction! But it wasn't my home anymore. My home is now in Newbridge.

My biggest thing is that I miss my friends. It's difficult at my age to establish a new circle of friends – because I'm not going into a job, for example. But I've joined the ICA and they organise outings. I've been to the Dáil for dinner! I'm going to join the flower club, too, and there's a couple of other things I want to check out. I was hairdressing from home before I moved to Ireland, and I was very fussy about my clients! They were all friends, and I do miss that. But I don't want to do that again – I swore to myself that I wouldn't go down that road. The work always creeps up on you. It ties you down.

Sometimes time hangs heavy. When I'm feeling fit, it doesn't. And I go away a lot – back to London, to Kerry, to Tyrone. I try not to get into too much of a routine. And I still keep in contact with my old life – I was at a wedding in Mayo recently, over a long weekend. The daughter of a woman I used to work with at the Irish club got married there. And there's lots of 'dos' like that all over the country; I can keep in touch with them all that way. It's a two-way thing, keeping in contact. I have to do my bit, too, and you can't let things go for too long either. It's difficult to get back in touch if there's been a gap.

Someone asked me recently if I was sorry that I hadn't made the move years ago. No. I'm not. I wouldn't have wanted to go ten, or even five years ago. I'm not one to wish I had done something, or I *hadn't* done something.

I've burnt my boats now! The timing was right.

'TIS A SAVAGE LOVE, THIS NATIVE SHORE'

Stephen Croghan, now in his mid-seventies, has a store of memories about his native Roscommon, dating back some fifty or sixty years. Although forced to leave Ireland through economic necessity, Stephen makes it very clear that, for him, emigration was merely an interruption in a life firmly rooted in the homeland. He is a gifted storyteller: his tales of rural Ireland in the forties and fifties illuminate the harsh realities of those decades and the reason why so many people felt forced to leave in search of something better.

Stephen, you've said that you can remember back to the forties when skilled workers were already leaving rural Ireland for England. What sort of details of that time have stayed with you?

There was an awful lot of skilled labour around Roscommon at that time – this would be 1939 – because Murphy's were building the County Hospital. That building went on for about three years. Then there was Ned Kelly, a contractor in Roscommon. He built the Christian Brothers' school up there, and he had a contract to build a lot of houses, but the war stopped that. So he had no work for all his crew.

As a result, there were all these skilled people queuing up to go to England for the construction. It was that or starvation. There was nothing to be got here. What they were getting at the labour exchange would buy nothing. All work on the building had stopped, and the only work to be had was on the land. That was a different sort of paid job altogether. You wouldn't get the likes of thirty bob from working on the land.

I remember a man called Cuddy, from Athleague, who owned a racing stables. Cuddy arrived at the labour exchange in Roscommon and started to sign up men for Wimpey and McAlpine in England.

He'd put a tag here on the coat, same as you'd tie a parcel, and up to the railway station with them. This fellow could be for Wrexby, so many fellows for London and so on. The name of the builder and the fellow's destination was on the tag. There was hundreds went out of this town like that, hundreds. As a matter of fact, I was talking to a man the other night and he'd painted for Wimpey. He's eighty now. Cuddy became a millionaire out of the commissions he got for supplying labour. That's how he bought his racing stables up in the Curragh. He was the first man in the Curragh to put in those swimming baths for the horses.

The people who stayed behind mostly worked on the land, and it was hard work, badly paid. I remember, when I was working outside Cork, there was two farm workers in the place and they had to hand-milk eighteen cows. They were up at six o'clock in the morning. They'd have to have the milking finished and the stables cleaned out again they got their breakfast. The can of milk had to be outside the gate by eight o'clock for collection. After that, they went to work on the land. Now, the only day they had no work on the land was a Sunday. But the cows still had to be milked on Sundays. I remember that their wages at that time was twenty-four shillings a week. They worked from six o'clock in the morning until six o'clock in the evening. They were living in an outhouse – they weren't even living in the house. They got their grub, but that was the wages: twenty-four bob. That's the way it was.

I remember too that you were only allowed half an ounce of tea a week. British people were allowed a quarter pound at that time. You could buy a pound of black-market tea below in the grocer's, smuggled in from the North, for twenty-eight shillings a pound. It was a fortune. Tom, the grocer, had a fellow in the North – an undertaker – and a doctor. Jim'd send up the hearse, the doctor would send the death certificate and the coffin-load of tea would cross the border.

Don't forget that a weekly wage then was only thirty bob – and that was for a top-skilled builder's labourer for a six-day week. There was no such thing as five days and tea breaks! That wasn't on the menu at all. All that was on that menu was work. You got your dinner break and that was it. And no half days either.

What work were you doing here, before you left for England?

I was blacksmithing for a fellow outside Cork city, a man called Bill Sheehan. When I started off with him I was only seventeen or eighteen, but I was already fully qualified to shoe horses. He paid me thirty bob for the first week.

'I'm not working for thirty shillings,' I told him. I was shoeing fifteen horses a day for him, sometimes sixteen. And, on top of that, I was up at seven o'clock in the morning, into the workshop at eight, didn't get my dinner until two. I worked until seven o'clock in the evening. It was a long day for thirty bob a week.

When I left Roscommon, I was getting fifteen shillings a set for shoeing a horse. The biggest horse that I'd shoe would be a Clydesdale. The material to shoe him only cost me two and sixpence. So out of each horse I'd have twelve and a tanner profit. With that twelve and sixpence I could buy a quarter ton of grade A English coal. You can shoe an awful lot of horses with a quarter ton of coal! In Cork, I was shoeing fifteen or sixteen horses for Sheehan per day, and he was getting twenty-four bob for each *one* of them.

Iron was scarce at that time, too. Sheehan was allowed a

hundredweight of iron a week, and that wasn't nearly enough for the horses he was doing. Every minute we got in between shoeing horses, we were making shoes. There'd be two thousand shoes on the wall. And you'd see them disappear. But as soon as they disappeared, more'd be going back up again. You weren't getting time to sit down and smoke. And Sheehan was sixty-five at that time – he wasn't doing a lot of the work! He'd redden the shoes in the fire, but I was the one doing all the sledging and using all the muscle power.

But the blacksmithing really disappeared after the War. What happened was, the government came along and opened up courses to teach people to become blacksmiths and farriers. Tom O'Connor from Dublin was a top man: he used to teach the engineers above in Bolton Street. And Tom was great at the charcoal sketches and landscapes, too. He did beautiful pastels. And he could certainly draw the horses – he'd draw the muscles and all. It'd be the very same as you'd see in a doctor's surgery; he really knew the horse's anatomy. That's what they were teaching then.

The farrier's territory is as far as the knee-joint on the horse. The vet shouldn't go below that. We had an old saying: 'If the horse is sore in his head, take off the shoe.' I saw my father and grandfather operate on the horses – they knew more than the veterinary surgeons. I saw them cut cancer growths out of a horse's throat, and the horse survived. I even watched them take a tooth out for an old farmer, Farmer Mahon! Made him rinse his mouth out with whiskey. There was no anaesthetic in those days, so they used the whiskey. There was no soreness after the whiskey.

Anyway, as I was saying, the blacksmithing really disappeared after the War. I had to get out of it because I didn't have the machinery to compete. I'd been trained in electric welding and lathe-turning on the government technical course, but sure, what was the point of being a welder when you'd no welding plant? What was the point of being a lathe-turner when you'd no lathe?

There was American aid to Europe at that time, to help mechanise the farmer. There were eleven blacksmiths that did the government course with me. I claimed that we came under the maintenance of agricultural machinery, which we did – we looked after the ploughs and the harrows down through the years. I said that if the farmer was going to be mechanised, then we were not equipped to maintain that machinery any longer, and that the work would go to garages and not to us. And that is what did happen. I applied to the Department of Industry and Commerce at that time for a grant to help me modernise. I was refused. They said I didn't come under their scheme. Then I applied to some other department, but I was told I didn't come under their scheme either.

I was very disillusioned. According to the government at the time, they wanted to keep the trades within the family. That's why they started these courses. But instead of keeping the trades alive, they drove people out of them. Anyway, I was very disappointed that I didn't get the government grant to modernise. Without it, I had nothing. I couldn't stay in Ireland. I had to go.

I got on to a TD here, Jack McQuillan, to push the case, but he never did. He wouldn't support me – said I was wrong. I felt very let down: I'd signed his nomination papers for two elections, and he was elected both times. But he did something once that I didn't agree with, so the third time he went up for election I wouldn't sign his nomination papers.

There was a by-election in Roscommon to fill Jimmy Burke's seat. He was Fine Gael and he'd always been a great politician for the people he represented – for everyone, no matter what party they supported. He gave away a lot of money to people who needed it, too. He supported his invalid sister, and her son and daughter.

What happened was, when Jimmy Burke died, his wife was put forward for election. Jack McQuillan also put forward a candidate, Oliver Macklin, a local solicitor. Macklin became a judge afterwards. Jack McQuillan got up in the square this day and made a speech in which he said 'This woman should be at home looking after her children.' I told him he'd just cut his political throat. That woman, I said, has nothing. I had seen Jimmy Burke selling the timber off his land, cutting down trees to help them survive. Mrs Burke had an invalid sister of Burke's to look after, and she had to feed and educate her own two children. 'That finishes you in politics,' I said to him. I was right.

In the next election, McQuillan was defeated and Mrs Burke won the seat hands down

At one stage, Jack McQuillan had been a great man for getting things done. For example, there were houses at the back of the railway station, big two-storey cottages, and all that was in them was dry toilets. Dr Noel Browne had just brought in the Health Act, so Jack McQuillan went up to the County Manager and gave him twenty-four hours to have the road bored and those houses connected to mains sewage. He threatened the County Manager that if the work hadn't started in twenty-four hours' time, he'd have him in front of the High Court. There was a digger there the next morning opening the road and the proper toilets were put in.

But there was no money in the country at that time, no money at all – this is the fifties I'm talking about.

When you left Roscommon to look for work, was that the first time you'd ever been to London?

It was. Even though I was thirty years of age, it was my first time outside Ireland. My sister was supposed to meet me at Euston. But I arrived and there was no one there. I said to myself that I'd better start working my own credentials here! So I went to the Tube and I looked at the map on the wall. The nearest station to where she lived was Earl's Court, so I bought my ticket and watched as the stations flew by. When I got to Earl's Court, I took the Cromwell Road exit. That was the back exit – the big stadium was across the road from that exit, the one where they do the boat shows, boxing matches, and all that.

There was a fellow selling papers outside the station so I asked him 'Where's Ifield Road?' 'Straight down there,' he says, 'across the junction there at the bottom.' I walked straight to her door and knocked. She got a quare surprise when I walked in! 'I could be standin' at Euston yet,' I told her.

Did you have difficulty finding work when you first arrived in London?

Yes, it wasn't easy. I was going back and forwards to the labour, and I'd almost run out of money, with train fares and bus fares and the like. There was always ten others before you for whatever job you wanted. And because you were an Irishman, you got nothing from the labour exchange. If you came from the British Commonwealth, somewhere like Jamaica, you would. But I was Irish, so I wasn't able to sign on. I got nothing. You worked or you starved, one or the other. I'd gone over with just a few quid in my pocket, and it was nearly all gone. So one day at the labour I said to the man 'Is there e'er a job at all?'

'Can you use a spade or a pick?' he says.

Says I 'I'll use anything as long as I get paid for it.'

That's all I wanted: wages. At this stage, I didn't care what I did. I'd pick stones. It was a case of having to. So he sent me to Brompton Cemetery and gave me a card to report in with. There was a firm there called White's of London.

'Righto,' I said. So off I went.

They were digging out these catacombs which were in the railway wall. Brompton Cemetery was bombed during the War. The people then took out the lead-lined coffins that were in the catacombs. They used the lead for bullets and buried all the debris out of the cemetery in the catacombs – I don't know where the bones were put. My sister told me that after the bombing headstones from the cemetery were found three streets away – and that was after they'd soared over the roofs of the three-storey houses on Ifield Road!

This wall around the cemetery was about thirty foot high, and the Brompton railway was the far side of it. The vibrations of the trains started to undermine the foundations of the wall. These catacombs were big rooms, about twelve foot high, with brick walls and a stone arch over the doorway. They were built maybe a couple of hundred years before, or more. At the top end, there were iron gates, and you could go straight through the middle of the catacombs originally. The coffins would be lined up on both sides, on shelves made of stone. So, that's where they packed all the debris after the bombing, just wheeled it into the catacombs and left it. But then the vibrations of the trains started to pack, pack, pack it and split the stone arch that was across the doorway. The wall actually started to move. So we had to remove the roof of the catacombs, which was made of twelve-foot slabs of stone. We broke those slabs with sledges into pieces and barrowed them to the road. They were then collected by lorry and used as filling on another site. There were eight or ten of us on that job. A Kerryman, I remember, and a young fella from Tipperary. Then there was Tom Dowdall from Dublin – his brother was a champion boxer. Tom had another light little fellow with him.

Anyway, I'd be smashing these stones with a sledge, and this light little fella would be firin' them into a barrow. And he'd say 'Didn't *we* do a good job?' We! And me the one with the twelve-pound sledge! I was a faster worker than most, and that didn't go down too well. When we knocked the top section, all that brick was used for hardcore, and it was put in a special place. We weren't allowed to get a blade of grass in the cemetery out of place. There was a kind of scaffolding put across the graves because we weren't allowed to walk across them with the barrow. The brickwork was dumped in one spot, the stonework in a different place because they were selling that.

So, when I finished up the first day, I had dug my first catacomb to twelve foot, to the floor, and one of the other men came up to me – his name was Crowley.

'Jaysus,' he said, 'you'd better stop what you're after doin'.' A real Corkman. 'Do you know what you're after doin'?' he asked me.

'What?' says I. 'What did I do wrong?'

He says 'You're after diggin' out a whole catacomb in a day. It took us,' he says, 'three days to dig the first one as a test, to see how long it would take.'

He wanted me to slow down!

In the cemetery, we got four and tuppence an hour. I knew nothing about the sub, that first day. I was as green as anything. By the evening, I didn't even have a smoke left.

The following morning a Kerry fellow asked me had I got the sub on the day before.

'What's that?' says I to him.

'Work the first day and you get thirty bob,' he said to me.

'That's the first I knew about it,' I said. Then I found out you'd get three pound the second day. So I went to the foreman.

'Didn't I give you the sub yesterday?' he said.

'No,' says I, 'because I didn't know what the sub was.'

'How much do you want?' he said to me. 'I'll give you whatever you want.'

So I asked him for a fiver. He offered me more, whatever I wanted. He wanted to make sure I'd be back.

'There's some you can give it to and some you can't,' was what he said to me.

I saw the Kerryman come in one morning after backing greyhounds. He'd won over three hundred pounds backing dogs. The next day, he hadn't the price of a box of matches. I said 'He'll never be able to go home to Ireland, the way he's going on.'

Then there was the young fellow from Tipperary. He used to go packing with Lyons's in the evening. He'd quit there at the cemetery, and then he'd go working all night. He'd be wall-fallin' and he coming into work in the morning. He'd be packing in Lyons's until about seven o'clock each morning.

Anyway, that job at the catacombs lasted just four or five weeks. I stayed with my sister all the time I was working in Brompton.

The next job I had was with Tom Watkins Engineers Ltd, in Richmond in Surrey. When I came looking for the job, I handed in my papers to the boss, the ones I had from the technical school. But that wasn't good enough for him.

'Do you know how to point picks?' he asks me. 'Do you know how to temper?'

'I do,' says I.

'Well,' he says, 'there's two picks.'

It was a test, because my job would be to forge all the iron for the lines. We used to do press parts for Compton Engineering, for the trains. We used to make the bars for the railway, too – the ones you'd use for shifting the line. We had all of those jobs subcontracted. The work on the bars was very precise – you weren't allowed to square the corners or take any short cuts that might weaken the bar. One part had to be three and one-eighth inches; but the other side had to be exactly three inches. There was no such thing as 'near enough'. Not on that job, not for the Englishman. For the Irishman, it was near enough, but not for this boss, not on this job.

And we'd make the hoists for telegraph poles, too, and send them off to Australia. We'd make them into six-, twelve- and eighteen-foot lengths. Steel poles, they were, sharpened to a pencil point at one end, and that fitted into an aluminium tube. That spike went into the ground; then, about three foot from the bottom of the pole, you had to make a handle. We used to make hundreds of them. Then we had to make the climbing irons for climbing the telegraph poles.

I'd be outside the gates at five to eight every morning; Charlie would then be the next one to arrive – he'd arrive on the spot of eight. I'd be getting the fires ready for Jim Miller and myself. Jim was working on one fire, and I'd be working on the other. That's where I met Jim: he's a Norfolkman, and we've been writing to each other for over forty years. Next thing, Bob Drey would arrive at nine o'clock – and he supposed to be there since eight! He was an electric welder – one of the best welders I ever met in my life. Then he'd start rolling cigarettes – it'd be half nine before he'd start to wake up. But if you got him on a job where there'd be numbers, he'd be brilliant. He used to make handles for a sort of a pump section, a double suction. Drey would start welding, and that's what you call a highly skilled job. He had to weld that tube around in a circle. Then he'd have so many holes bored and a handle on both sides for the pump. You would never get a break in that weld: you would never know where he had started and where he had finished. And there'd be no cleaning up on it. He was brilliant at it, a real craftsman. We used to get a couple of thousand of those jobs – subcontracted from another fellow.

Now, Jim Miller – he was a brilliant gas welder. Oxyacetylene. You couldn't get better. He'd be cutting steel out of block, where we'd be making jaws for twisting wires together. He'd cut the steel just like he was cutting glass. There'd be no rough bits anywhere. All you'd have to do was give it a rub on the stone and it would be perfectly smooth.

The work we did was all skilled, highly skilled. There was no room for mistakes, no half measures, not for our boss.

You met your wife while you were working in London, isn't that right?

Yes, I met Mary in London. Meeting her was an accident, you know. I was having a drink with her father one night, and Mary was on her way to meet him, just in case he wouldn't get home safe! Her parents were both Irish, her father from Kerry and her mother from Wexford, but she was born in London. We got married in London in Our Lady of Victories, Kensington. We had to get married in the crypt because the church had been bombed during the War.

After our honeymoon in Ireland, she had to go back to London without me. I had tonsillitis and the doctor wouldn't let me travel. But Mary had to go back for work – she worked in a savings bank.

I miss her terribly, now. She was a keen gardener, loved her garden. She was a terror to read, too. She had me and all the children signed into the library. Up they went, every week, from the time they were that height. She used to read five books a week, herself. And if ever she didn't have time to read them, she got them on tape. She'd work away with them on in the background. She was Treasurer of the ICA [Irish Countrywomen's Association] and she used to organise the tours for them – bus tours, tours to the Japanese Gardens, tours all over the country. She was always looking for a bargain, and no matter where she went she'd come back with one, I can guarantee you that.

When I did go back to London after the wedding, a fortnight after Mary, I remember that there were twelve young girls on the boat, all of them from around here in Roscommon. They were going nursing. When we arrived at Euston, they hadn't a clue where they were going. One of them was going to Essex, and the rest of them were going to a hospital in London.

When I got off the train, I called over the Salvation Army people and I said 'I leave this young girl in your charge. Make sure she gets on the train for Essex.' Then I got back on the train again and I brought the other eleven to the station where they were to get off – there was people there waiting for them, representatives from the hospital. Then I'd to get back on the train again and go back to Earl's Court! I didn't want them to get lost. They were country girls, and it was their first time in London.

You didn't mix much in the established Irish communities like Kilburn and Cricklewood, did you?

No, no, no, no, no – I didn't get into that. I saw a lot of what was going on. Jim Miller and myself went to a pub one night for a few drinks. There were a lot of Irish in it. They started up all these rebel songs. That didn't go down too well with Jim, now. He'd been in the Navy, and he'd served for a short time in the North of Ireland. He was the sort of a fellow who said that Britain should give back the Six Counties. They don't own it, he'd say. It belongs to ye. But what was going on inside the pub that night nettled him. 'Now,' he said, 'they should have a little bit more respect. They're getting a good living here.' And that was my point of view, too. There was nothing left for them in Ireland at that time, and they *were* getting a good living in England.

But the Irish didn't have too good a reputation around Notting Hill Gate and up that country. There were several murders around there at that time, between the Irish and the blacks. The blacks were pimping for the Irish girls, the prostitutes, and that didn't go down too well. I kept away from that country as much as possible – I wasn't too fond of it at all, I can tell you.

I was friends with all sorts of people – I didn't feel the need to be among Irish all the time. Jim Miller was always a great friend to me. When I went back to England for another spell in the early sixties when things weren't great here, he insisted I stay with him and his wife. He wouldn't hear of me going anywhere else. Jim's wife wouldn't charge me anything for my keep, so I did a bit of building for them in their house.

His wife was a Welsh woman and, at one time, she had worked for Jameson's in Dublin, the whiskey crowd. Then she became seamstress to Sarah Churchill, Churchill's daughter. They were both very kind people, Jim and his wife, very good to me.

I get annoyed when I hear people giving out about England – why wouldn't I? Didn't they get a good living there? Mind you, I always knew I'd never stay in England. I always knew I'd come home. ''Tis a savage love, this native shore.'

Uncles of mine went to America and never came back. They had a huge livery business there. Then they got the contract for

United Dairies in Newport. Five blacksmiths out on the road now, mobile forges, moving from ranch to ranch. It's a big business. They never came home.

But I was always determined that I would. I've never regretted coming back.

When you did come back in the early sixties, were things that much better for you than they had been?

I still had to go back and forwards to London for work – that was when I stayed with Jim Miller and his wife. I went back and worked for a firm making pipes for the Thames gas. There were two thousand men working there.

To get back in when you came back to Ireland – that was the thing. So that people knew you were there and ready to work. My family were at this trade for generations. I can trace them all back, all blacksmiths. My grandfather had seven brothers – one of them was a coachsmith to McGattigan's in Athlone. He had a coachworks of his own at one time, in Clara, and he had two sons working for him, Stephen and Luke. Another son, Paddy, got the VC and the DSM in the 1914–18 War. He came back and worked on the railways in Athlone after the War. Then Stephen and Luke fell out with the father. He would often go off on the beer, and the two sons might have forty tyres ready but they daren't even put one on unless he was there. He was the boss; they could do nothing without him, so they bailed out.

The two of them went to the Clyde in England, one as a ship's blacksmith and the other as a ship's painter. Stephen was transferred from the Clyde to Harland and Wolff, and he was working in Belfast in 1928 with a young Orangeman as an apprentice. The Orangeman tipped him off: he said 'You'd better get out of Belfast before the night is out.' Stephen was living on the Falls Road. He had to pack his bag, himself and the wife, and flee with the two children. There were twenty-eight houses burned on the Falls Road that night.

So Stephen came back to Athlone and ended up as a blacksmith in the Irish Army.

My father was a brilliant blacksmith, too brilliant. He couldn't settle down to it. He went through hard times. I don't think my mother was behind him enough. You need the backing. He died young, too young. He was sixty-five; my mother was eighty-five. My father knew more about horses and doctoring horses – and even human beings – than anyone else I've ever known. People would make appointments to see him from all over. People came to have their teeth pulled, or their corns done.

There was a man called Watt, who used to preach in the local church. He came to have his corns done. My father would put him sitting on a chair, with a cushion under him.

'Don't draw the blood, Tom!' was all you'd hear. My father used to take a hold of the corn and a cut-throat razor. He'd cut the corn clean out, and no blood anywhere. He'd a very delicate touch for a man his size. He hadn't the big hands you'd expect from a blacksmith. Those hands forged more iron and shod more horses than any other man I know. He told me himself that he was only eleven years of age when his father sent him to shoe the horses for Cootes of Carraroe.

His day's work started at the break of dawn, and he worked until dusk. There was a man taken off the land to sledge for him, and he'd shoe sixteen horses, as well as doing the other ironwork around Lord Goff's estate that needed to be done. Hangers for gates, things like that. The man who was sledging, his day's wages was tuppence. My father's day's pay was seven and sixpence. At that time, he told me, you'd get a pint of Guinness for tuppence, or a pound of American bacon. My grandfather sent him there to shoe the horses, while his other two brothers worked the forge.

My grandfather was farrier to Lord Crofton, and there were an awful lot of racing stables around Roscommon at that time which aren't there now. There was Mulligan's, where the racetrack is now, and Laddy Nealon's of Stone Park – they had a point-to-point course there. There was another point-to-point out on Lord Crofton's land as well. Lord Crofton's land stretched from a mile outside Roscommon – there was a big pair of iron gates going in there – to Moate Park house, to another set of gates at Ballymurray, and then the last pair of gates at Knockroghery. Knockroghery is where Lord Crofton had the point-to-point course. Then there were the trainers, the Farmers and the O'Malleys. So there was plenty of work for blacksmiths.

But that all finished after the War. Then when I came back from London and the petrol started to be available again, in the early sixties, there were fewer and fewer horses. Things were all right until the petrol started to flow again!

But it's a great trade nowadays, looking after the racehorses.

I used to shoe thoroughbreds for a man called Tom Shaughnessy. Now, Tom was a bit of a seer. If a mare was in foal, or a woman was pregnant, Tom would be able to tell whether the child would be a boy or a girl. I remember he had a young fella working for him one time, and he said to the boy's mother 'You'd better get a miraculous medal and put it around that young fella's neck.' Six weeks later, the young fella went to Ballyshannon, but he never arrived home.

Everyone was out looking for him. Shaughnessy said 'You'll find him in a wood with a cord around his neck.' They found him in Moate wood, with binder twine around his neck. And he only after parting from a pal of his, he had only walked about a half a mile. He'd killed himself and nobody knew why. And Shaughnessy had foreseen it. It's a strange gift; I don't know that I'd want it.

What are the differences between the skills of a blacksmith and those of a farrier?

Don't forget the blacksmith works in iron, but the farrier has to know all the bone structure of the foot. The blacksmith might know how to nail on a shoe, but that would be it. It's a rough job. But the farrier has to know about sidebones, for example, and how to make a proper shoe, a special shoe, for a horse with that condition. A sidebone on a horse comes from oxidisation – too much lime salts in the land. The cartilage attached to a small bone in the hoof is turned into bone. Some people believed that the sidebone comes from the mare that bred the horse, but that's not so: it comes from oxidisation. A farrier has to know that and how to fix that.

Do you have any sense of sadness that all the skills you acquired are no longer in your family?

I do. I learned a lot of these things from my father – I watched him all through my childhood. He used to shoe racehorses and he wouldn't even need to measure for the shoe: he'd just know by looking at the horse what he needed.

All that knowledge was passed on from generation to generation in my family. I'm sad that all that skill has come to an end. None of my sons wanted to continue the trade – they knew it was hard graft and the pay didn't come easy. Working for yourself, you depend on others to pay up when the job is done. But the money's not always forthcoming when you need it. Young people want wages at the end of each week, not living from hand to mouth like long ago.

But that's modern Ireland for you. Sure look at us now: what happens if the oil stops? It did the last time, in the seventies. What will this country do then?

There's no young man now that knows how to use a horse and plough.

GALTYMORE CRICKLEWOOD

SUN TONIGHT 5th DEC

MAGNIFICENT

MIAMI
SHOWBAND

WITH THE DARLING
DICKIE ROC

SUN   12th DEC

GENE
STUART

MIGHTY AVONS

Please do not throw this handbill on the road or footpath

Printed by Connaught Lithoservices Ltd. Tel: 01-731 0900

GALTYMORE CRICKLEWOOD

SUN TONIGHT 30th APR

D.J.
AND THE
KERRY BLUES
FOUR BAND SENSATION

SAT   6th MAY

BRENDAN SHINE
SHOWBAND

FOUR BAND FEAST

SUN   7th MAY
TONY KENNY
AND THE
SANDS
IRELANDS LIKEABLE AND LIVELY BAND

Please do not throw this handbill on the road or footpath

Printed by Connaught Lithoservices Limited Tel. 01-731 0900

'THE ONLY SIN, IT SEEMED, WAS BREAKING THE SIXTH OR THE NINTH COMMANDMENT'

Fr Seamus Fullam, from Co. Longford, has worked among the Irish in London for almost five decades. With five years to retirement, Fr Fullam looks back on his life experience among the Irish in London and confronts some of the difficulties facing him in 'coming home'.

How did your work with the Irish in London begin?

When I came over first, I went to a late-vocation college in Osterley, Middlesex, called Campion House. There were about one hundred and fifty of us there from every walk of life and about fifteen to twenty per cent of us, I think, would have been Irish. Most of the people there had had other careers beforehand – some were from the Army, some had studied medicine, some had worked on the buses; about half would have been converts from other denominations, predominantly the Anglican faith.

I was a 'late' vocation in the sense that I didn't begin my studies until I was nineteen. People generally went into the Seminary, or Novitiate, much earlier – perhaps at sixteen or seventeen. I did a two-year course in Campion House to learn Latin and then went on to join a community called the Oblates of Saint Charles. Their main base was in Bayswater – Saint Mary of the Angels in Bayswater. My fellow students and I didn't go to the Seminary then – it was a different system for us. We did a course with the Franciscans in a place called East Bergholt, about six miles from Ipswich. We did a course in Philosophy there for two years, followed by four years of Theology.

Once my pastoral work began, I always worked among the Irish – the Bishop of the diocese's decision was that I was sent to predominantly Irish parishes. My first parish was Saint Mary of the Angels in Bayswater, where I stayed for ten months. Then I was changed to a place called Bosworth Road in North London. During subsequent years I went back to Bayswater again, then Euston, then Saint Paul's in Wood Green and then to East Acton where I worked for just under ten years.

One is generally appointed to a parish for ten to twelve years. I'd another ten years at Grahame Park and, finally, I was moved to St Patrick's here in West Hendon, and I've been here for six years.

I think it's unfair for a priest to be left for thirty years in the same parish – unfair to the priest and unfair to the people. It might be someone the parishioners don't want – and then they can't get rid of him! So I never had any hesitation in accepting the moves, although it does get harder as you get older. It's more difficult to pull up the roots: they go down deeper as you grow older. But the moving from place to place gave me great experience in dealing with all sorts of people and their different problems.

As I've said, all the parishes I've worked in have been predominantly Irish. Those Irish I met were people who had to leave home because there was nothing there for them. They came over on the boat with nothing. I remember a few times myself travelling over in the cattle boat in the company of emigrants. The cattle were put in underneath and the passengers travelled on top.

What would you identify as the most difficult challenges that the Irish faced in the 1950s on their arrival in London?

Culture shock.

Everything was so completely different from what they were used to at home. They had to find solutions to many problems, often without help, in some areas of their lives. Many got into difficulties because of loneliness. Even though people lived in blocks of flats surrounded by others, they were often very lonely. They ended up spending all their money in the pub, or they made unsuitable marriages and fell away from the Church. Some of the Irish were very lucky in that they met caring landladies. They were only young fellows, and these landladies mothered them. Others weren't so lucky.

The Church tried to help out, both with the social clubs and with other, more practical difficulties. I remember on one occasion during the fifties, there was heavy snow which lasted for a good many months, so there was no work to be had. A priest by the name of Fr Dore, from Quex Road Church in Kilburn, helped out as best he could during that time. He got the men to clear away the snow from around the church. He paid them a couple of pounds, whatever he could, and that was a lot of money in those days. He did that for weeks and weeks. And he wasn't the only one; other parishes did their best, too, and the Saint Vincent de Paul was very good at helping out those who had fallen on hard times.

However, there was one big problem which most young Irish men had to face, and that was isolation. They would come home from work, get their dinner and then have to sit there looking at the four walls. There was no television, maybe just a radio. They were people who weren't used to reading, and so the natural thing was to go out to the pub, to seek out company. And that brought problems. In many parishes, the Church came up with the idea to form social clubs so that after work, and particularly at weekends, the men could come and play games of cards or darts and socialise with other people. Many marriages were made between men and women who met at the Catholic social clubs.

Those clubs were a tremendous asset to people for many years and helped them in a lot of ways. And the clubs also kept them in contact with the Church and their duties. As a result, many people became involved with the Saint Vincent de Paul and the Legion of Mary. Every parish I've ever been in, eight out of every ten collectors at Sunday Mass are Irish, or of Irish descent. Nowadays, of course, the whole ethos of the Catholic social clubs has changed. The young person today is not interested in the old songs like 'Lovely Leitrim'! Now they want discos and Karaoke and that sort of thing. It's a different approach now and that's why many of the clubs in the local parishes have closed down.

We're lucky still to have ours here in West Hendon. And that's because Shelagh Kane, who manages the club, is able to get great bands to come and play there. For example, a few weeks ago, we had Sean Cassidy: popular acts still bring in the crowds on a Saturday night. On Sundays, once the GAA championships begin, we have the wide screen, Setanta. The big screen brings a lot of people back to watch the matches but, again, it's the older generation, not the younger people.

In my experience, those men and women who came over in the fifties had a great respect and a great feeling for their parents. There was a great bond between parent and child. The grown-up children had huge respect for what their parents had gone through for them and that's why the five- or ten-shilling postal order kept going home, well into the sixties. If the father or mother was sick, they would go back to Ireland several times in order to look after them. They kept that contact until the parents died.

But increased affluence and secularism, both here and in Ireland, have interfered with family life. Now, I don't see that bond that there used to be. I think that when people have tough times, it unites them. If things are too handy, that bond doesn't happen so easily.

In what other, practical ways did the Church help the Irish in London?

I believe that the Church did everything it could to help the Irish here in the 1950s – very much so. For example, because of the culture in Ireland – and I'm not blaming the Church or the government or any individuals for that – but because of the culture, if a girl got pregnant outside of marriage she had to disappear overnight. In the Ireland of the 1950s, it appears that there was only the one sin. The Church authorities tended only to stress the sixth and ninth commandments: a fellow could come home drunk, beat up his wife, kick her out of bed, but the only sin, it seemed, was breaking the sixth or the ninth commandment. For the Day of Judgement, there's nothing mentioned about the sixth or the ninth: 'When I was hungry, did you feed me? When I was thirsty, did you give me to drink? When I was sick or in prison, did you come to visit me?'

There were other sins which should have been stressed, both sins of omission and commission, sins against real, genuine love of your neighbour. For example, there was what was called the 'spiking of land'. It was a practice widespread in some rural areas. You'd have a row with your neighbour, and, in revenge, you'd place irons all around his meadow. When he came to cut the grass, the blades of the machine would be damaged beyond repair. There were also incidents where the tongue of the donkey was tied so that it couldn't eat. As the problem was a hidden one, the animal would die without anyone knowing what was wrong with it. Or people would steal each other's turf at night – all very serious sins, involving the livelihood of others, and they were never spoken about! Never even mentioned. There was only the one sin in 1950s Ireland.

And because of the emphasis of the Church authorities in those days, all that negativity was projected onto the poor girls who found themselves pregnant outside marriage. They had to leave the country – the shame was so great. You could be a thief, or a drunkard – but your sin was rarely mentioned. Once those girls made their escape and came to London, they'd be put in touch with us and we'd send them on to the Crusade of Rescue. This was an organisation which helped and cared for girls in crisis. Monsignor Flood and Bishop Craven, along with others, added credibility to the Crusade. It was mostly women who ran it – they could talk more easily to other women – and they were terrific. The Crusade helped those girls who had to give their babies up for adoption. Nine out of ten mothers went for adoption because they simply couldn't go home with their babies. Sometimes, adoptions took place without any paperwork: they were arranged privately. It's great to see that girls today are able to keep their babies, that they don't have to give them away.

In those days, too, we used to have people from the Legion of Mary to meet the girls off the train at Euston. They were terrified at their predicament, but they couldn't stay at home. That was the culture and the outlook of most people at that time. Usually, the girl's mother would be more understanding, but the father was often unChristian. They kicked their daughter out, and that was it. Sometimes, they got physical with the daughter and were extremely violent. Some poor girls never went home. Somehow, it was always their fault. The men got away with it.

I remember hearing a story from a Canon at home. He had a very dry sense of humour. This young girl had been sent away to have her baby, and the mother told everyone she'd gone to have her appendix out. The Canon told me afterwards that he had seen the young girl out for a walk one day and she was 'pushing the appendix in a pram!'

Do you think that the Irish worked hard in London in the fifties?

Those that I met, for the most part, worked hard and were glad to have work. There are always people who are shy of work, but they were in the minority at that time. Most of the people I knew would always send home ten shillings every week, or whatever they could afford, to their mother and father. Some of the Irish did very well indeed, and returned home to buy farms or build bungalows. There were those Irish who 'made it' and moved on to good areas here and became more integrated into the English way of life. But no matter where they moved to, I've found that they form the backbone of every parish where they live – that's what I experienced in all the parishes I've been in. But, of course, there were those who came upon lean times, too. Very often it wasn't their own fault – they just couldn't handle their situation.

There were also the others, of course, who got themselves into trouble, trouble of their own making. Because of the loneliness, they spent too much time in the pub and became addicted to drink. That led to some of them becoming involved in a life of crime. Prison visitors would tell you that many of those who ended up in prison at that time were Irish.

Sometimes, too, there were unrealistic expectations of what life in London could offer. I know so many fellows who'd go back to Ireland for Christmas and they'd pull a twenty quid note out of their pocket and treat everybody in the pub to a drink. Then they'd take out another one. That was a lot of money in those days, an awful lot of money. Other fellows watching this, earning very little in Ireland, would think that the streets of London were paved with gold. They'd come over to London, get into difficulties and then they were too shy to go back home. They would often come to the priest for help, and then I'd get their story. They'd come to London believing that they would get handy money; then they realised they had to work hard, often in really difficult conditions on the buildings.

Very often, the people who were the hardest on them were the Irish themselves – they made the worst foremen. I remember, in one case, the nastiest foreman was from the same county as the men working under him. He used to lay into them in particular –

men from his own corner of the world. Some of those foremen were tyrants, shouting at the men. Once they got into a position of authority, they wanted to throw their weight around, usually to cover up some inadequacy or sense of inferiority of their own. Whereas those Englishmen who came up the hard way were much more understanding of people. Many of the men I met through the Catholic club told me they were delighted when they got an Englishman as their foreman. I spoke to an Irishman once who'd spent his whole life in England working on the buildings. He told me that he had never met an unpleasant English foreman.

There were some firms, owned now by Irishmen, that got rich on the back of exploiting their own.

And of course nowadays it's the Irish who are picking up the Latvian and Lithuanian workers outside the Crown in Cricklewood, and basically doing to others what was done to them: showing the same lack of compassion.

Are the majority of your parishioners settled here for life?

A lot of people have gone back to Ireland. I like to tell people that since I came here to St Patrick's, six years ago, we've 'lost' about two hundred and thirty-four parishioners. It took the American and the British Army to shift Saddam and his men – had they sent me, I'd have got rid of the lot of them by myself!

Those people who have been able to go home to Ireland have all done well. I have very few weddings here now, but each year I do about a dozen sets of papers for people to get married at home in Ireland. Young people have told me that if they want to get married at home on a Saturday, they have to make a booking up to three years beforehand. The pound is so strong against the euro that they can afford to go back and get married there, and good luck to them.

In all the parishes I've worked in, I've found that the second-generation Irish are very conscious of their background and they go to Ireland to spend their holidays there. No matter how long an Irish person is out of the home place, they'll always say 'I'm going *home* for Christmas.' People routinely ask me was I *home* for the summer, and I'll say 'Yes, I was home.'

However, settling back into Ireland as a returning emigrant can be very difficult. I think that jealousy is something inherent in the Irish temperament, the Celtic temperament. You meet with a great deal of jealousy in Irish people, in all walks of life. There can be huge resentment of other people who do better, particularly with regard to material riches. I hear that today, from people who go back to Ireland to settle. They're greeted with 'You're only a blow-in!' That sort of begrudgery raises its head from time to time here, too, among the Irish. When I'm talking to people about those families who are planning to go back to Ireland, I'll hear 'Well, I wouldn't be bothered going back. You're not welcome there.' Or else they'll say, 'Well, they won't be too long there before they're back again.'

You go back to Ireland twice a year. What sort of changes have you noticed over the years?

You just cannot compare Ireland now and the Ireland I left fifty years ago. The first thing that strikes me every time I fly into Dublin is the amount of cranes I see everywhere. Where you see cranes you see plenty of employment. It means there's building going on, and, once the building is a success, everything else follows. I see where once there was a small little hardware shop, now there'll be two – and they're not small any longer either.

When I left Longford fifty years ago, you could look down the street every Thursday and Friday and see everyone's ass and cart tied at the side of the road. Now you'd have to go to Connemara, I suppose, to see an ass. Today, as far as the eye can see, there are cars everywhere – all the best of cars: Opels, several Mercs. Two or three to each household – everybody has to have one. Go to the car park in Longford and you won't see even one banger. Young people today have so much money, whereas we had nothing.

But affluence hasn't stopped the rise in crime. Some years ago, I was passing through Dublin and parked my car close to the Pro-Cathedral. I wasn't long away, but when I came back, the car window had been broken. I used to smoke at that time – it's a good many years ago, in fact. Anyway, a bottle of whiskey and two hundred cigarettes were stolen on me. I couldn't understand it – the car was parked in a very public place. There was a Garda nearby and he told me that I was dead lucky. I was driving an English-registered car and he told me the thieves would soon come back to do the boot! He showed me where to go to get the window repaired. On my way in, there was a fellow coming out – his windscreen had been done – and yet another followed, with all his windows broken. I was telling this story to a man I know at home – he was a local businessman. His car had been broken into somewhere in Dublin, but they couldn't drive it away because the immobiliser kicked in. So they wrecked it; just wrecked it. I don't go near Dublin now.

I was commenting recently to a colleague that in Ireland affluence has brought big problems. He reminded me of the Philosophy we'd studied many years ago under the Franciscans. Our teacher, Fr Jude Kidd, taught us that affluence was divisive.

If you've no religion, there's a vacuum in your life. So many people are unaware of that vacuum and of the fact that that can only be filled by God. So football becomes the religion, or cricket or sex. I notice in Ireland that so many young people don't go to Mass anymore. The scandals in the Catholic Church haven't helped. Young people don't feel the need for God in their lives, so the vacuum is filled for them by fast cars, lots of money, good jobs. I know that this is a great worry for parents in Ireland, but I always say that you can't force young people to worship God – they must do so freely. The ordinary human being was made for God, as Saint Augustine said, and only God will satisfy that longing in the heart. Those who have no religion here, in England, are not aware of that fact.

And young people in Ireland aren't aware of that longing either – the God-shaped hole is filled by all the other things that affluence brings. Those who attend Mass in Ireland now are the older generation. But it's the times we live in. Perhaps as young people grow older and more mature they will realise what is missing in their lives. 'You have made us for Yourself, oh Lord, and our hearts are restless and ever ill at ease until they rest in You' – that's what it's like until the longing for God is fulfilled.

The rise in the rate of suicide is another indication of that vacuum in people's lives, too. I say Masses for young men who are victims of suicide – and nine times out of ten, it's men. Poor fellows who drown themselves, or hang themselves; usually it's young men between eighteen and twenty-eight. And the people left behind are baffled: but he had a great job, a lovely car and all that. It's a dreadful heartbreak for the mother and father, but, if the vacuum is that desolate a place to be, young men see no other way out for themselves. I deal with incidents like this with families from all over.

What has been the most fulfilling part of your work among the Irish over your long career?

Administering the sacraments to them, I think. But I'm also very conscious of the times that I've failed them. As one gets older, one becomes more aware of how one failed people in the past. Things that I should have done, I didn't do, so I don't like to mention the positives. We all make mistakes when we're young, and those mistakes can come back to haunt you. If I was able to help one or two along the way, that's good.

I was ordained over forty years ago to help people – that was my role. On the fortieth occasion of my ordination, I concelebrated Mass with Cardinal Cormac Murphy-O'Connor and some other priests. I didn't want any other sort of celebration, because I was simply doing the job I was ordained for. Perhaps with another job it would be different. But I wanted to keep the date quiet and have no fuss.

I have about four hundred and eighty parishioners now – there were about seven hundred before I came, but I've sent them all home, back to Ireland! I don't know them all personally, but I know most of them to see. I say five Masses at the weekends – two on Saturday and three on Sunday, and I see most of them then. The problem is, I'm hopeless at remembering names.

This church used to be the school hall and it became the parish church in 1964. It was needed to take the overspill from the parish of Hendon up the road – so many Irish came here in the fifties and sixties. And that's the way it has been since the Famine – the Irish have brought the faith all over the world with them. Out of the evil of the Famine came good, and people tend to forget that. Look at the Irish names in the hierarchy of the Latin American church, for example.

The profile of this area is changing now. Kilburn and Cricklewood are just down the road, and we're all part of the one community, really. But now the Irish are leaving. Muslims have become a large part of the community and we have a mosque just across the road. As the Irish move out, the Asian population are buying up the property. In twenty years or so, if the trend continues, it will no longer be a predominantly Irish community.

Both communities are very similar in that the Irish tend to stay among themselves, and the Asians tend to stay among themselves. It's an issue which I had to deal with over the years in the Club. I did not like people referring to 'The Irish Catholic Club' – it's not; the Club was always intended for everyone. Of the people who came, 99.9 per cent were Irish, but we didn't intend that: that's what happened. People like to stay within their own cultures.

West Hendon is still a working-class area, like all the parishes

I've worked in – with the possible exception of Bayswater. My natural sympathies lie with those people, and there's no point in sending a priest to somewhere that he's out of place.

I'm personally very hurt about all the upheavals in the Catholic Church over the last number of years. I can understand priests getting involved with women – it's the most natural thing in the world – but it galls me to think that a priest, who is supposed to be a trusted man, can abuse a little child. It's quite simply beyond me. They do such damage. And it's a terrible thing when a man uses a family to get to a child.

I was at home in Ireland during the height of a local scandal involving children. I'd adopt a very low profile and wear an open-necked shirt to avoid attention when I went out.

There isn't the same amount of scandal at all in the English Catholic Church – the odd one, from time to time – but it has affected all of us very badly. When I go to schools now, I say to the Head teacher could he or she accompany me when I go to the yards where the children are playing. Teachers are suffering, too. Before this, if a child was upset or hurt, you could take them up and cuddle them – but there's no way we, or teachers, can do that now. Besides that, there's always the fear that if a child doesn't like you, or if their parent doesn't like you, all they have to do is accuse you of something inappropriate. Once you're accused here you have to leave straightaway, which is very unfair.

I was told recently to leave the Sacristy door wide open so that I could be seen from the church. A little girl came in and I shot out to do some work on the altar, waiting until other people arrived so that I wouldn't be seen to be alone with her. It's all very shocking, really, for all of us who work in any way with children.

Do you hope to go home to Ireland to retire?

Please God. If I live that long. The bank manager and myself own a bungalow there, you see! I'd bought it for my mother so that she could be near the church and the doctor. She died some years ago and I kept it on.

But there's no way I'll retire until the whole Commission of Inquiry has investigated all the cases of alleged child abuse in Ireland. I wouldn't feel comfortable being at home until all the accusations of paedophilia are out in the open and dealt with.

I've another five years to go before I retire. Please God, by that time, I'll be able to go home in peace.

'HELPING THOSE YOUNG PREGNANT GIRLS BECAME MY MISSION IN LIFE'

Sheila Dillon (not her real name) is a woman in her early seventies. She exudes warmth and compassion, and she continues to work energetically for the good of her local community. She dedicated herself to looking after others during her long career as a nurse. She has chosen to remain anonymous, lest any of her reminiscences be hurtful to others. To respect that wish for anonymity, all the names of people mentioned during our interview have been changed.

You trained as a general nurse in Manchester in 1949 and then specialised in plastic surgery for two years before moving to London. Tell me about the incident which changed the course of your nursing life.

Well, one day when I was crossing the road on my bike, a lady ran out of one of the nearby houses, shouting, waving her arms, and she stopped me in my tracks. I had my storm cap on, so she thought I was a nurse. *I* thought I was a nurse at that time, too – but I wasn't the sort of nurse she needed! I mean, I was fully qualified, knew all about plastic surgery and all the rest of it, but I was no use to her at all. She was just about to have her baby – and I hadn't the remotest idea, not even a clue, of what to do to help her.

'I'm going to have my baby, I'm going to have my baby.' That's all she kept saying. So I got off my bike and did the only thing I could think of. I put my hand up and stopped a passing motorist. We were on the edge of one of those new council estates that were being built after the War, and cars were whizzing around everywhere.

'Excuse me,' I said, 'but can you take this lady across to the hospital?'

The driver just looked at me, but I wouldn't let him off the hook. All I wanted was to get this woman to Walpole Green Hospital. There was a friend of mine there, Mary Ruane, that had been a midwife in my general hospital, and I knew that she would look after this poor woman and her baby. Anyway, the man took her to the hospital – as a matter of fact, I was there before him because I'd flown over on my bicycle. I grabbed a chair from the Casualty Department, sat the woman down and whizzed away off to Ward 14, where Mary worked.

'Mary, Mary, come quickly!' I said. 'There's a woman out here and she's just about to have her baby!'

'All right, all right,' said Mary, 'just be calm and bring the trolley.'

I went charging down the ward. Nurses are only supposed to run in cases of fire or haemorrhage. Well, there was no fire, but I was terrified there might be a haemorrhage. In the meantime, Mary had taken the woman into the examination room and put her on the couch. That woman had been dead right when she said the baby was coming – when I arrived minutes later with the trolley, there was Mary with this infant in her arms and he roaring like a bull!

We waited for the placenta and I thought I had never seen such a mess in my life. But I was delighted – even though it wasn't my delivery, I felt I had played my part. The next day I went to see our Matron, Anne Moore – a lovely woman from Newry, Co. Down. I told her I wanted to hand in my notice. She was shocked.

'Sister,' she said, 'what are you talking about?'

'Look,' I said, 'I thought I was a nurse – but now I know I'm bloody well not.' I told her about the incident of the day before and said that, but for Mary Ruane, a young woman and her baby could have died. I was supposed to be a nurse, and I hadn't been able to do a thing about it. I had decided, I said, to do midwifery.

'Okay,' she said, 'and when you finish your midwifery, come back to us.'

Off I went to Davyhulme and did the first part of my midwifery – that took six months. We were supposed to have had ten deliveries under our belt before we did our exams but, thanks be to God, I had a lot more than ten. Once I finished my midwifery, I went back to Withenshaw for one more stint and nursed patients with tuberculosis, which was another kind of nursing that I'd always been interested in. After that, I suppose the wanderlust set in and I came down to London, initially to Moorfields Eye Hospital, in 1959.

You found nursing in London a very different experience from Manchester. Why was that? What made this new departure in your career so special?

I wasn't interested in staying in Moorfields, spending my days putting drops in people's eyes. I was looking around, waiting for whatever new course might take my interest. I did a bit of private nursing once I got my OND, and then I went off to take a look at Maida Vale hospital – it was a branch of the National Hospital for Nervous Diseases. I signed on there for two weeks, but at the end of those two weeks the desire for doing more courses had suddenly vanished: it was as though I had finally found my place.

Maida Vale was a hospital that I had never seen the like of in my life. It was a wonderful place to work. There was an old Matron there who went around with a little bow under her chin. But that woman was one special human being. I had never seen anyone like her. She would come around on the Sunday morning and greet all of the patients individually.

'Good morning, Eileen. How are you today? And how is your

little boy?' Or 'Good morning, Jean, are you well today? And is your husband out of hospital yet?'

She had a word for everybody – knew everybody's name; there was none of this stiff formality that you often get. She was genuinely interested in every patient under her care. Maida Vale was a very specialised hospital, and people would travel long distances to see the patients on a Sunday. I could have six or seven visitors in the day room having their dinner, which you weren't supposed to do, of course. I'd just ask those patients who were confined to the hospital how many visitors they were expecting at the weekend, and I'd make sure that everybody was catered for with a decent meal.

Anyway, one Sunday the Matron pulled up in her 'Pink Goddess', her Triumph car, at dinner time and I thought to myself 'Oh, Christ, I'm for it now.'

She had broken her hip a long time beforehand, but she still used a stick. I went out to help her and as we passed the day room, I just said casually 'There are a few people in there that have just travelled up from Cardiff; they're having their dinner.'

'I should think so, too,' she said, firmly.

And that was that – she'd rather that people had a good dinner after their long journey than waste all that food. There is so much food wasted in hospitals, it isn't true. Feed the visitors, and never mind the rules. She was a thoroughly good woman. It was a fantastic hospital to work in. I stayed there for thirty years.

Irish women went nursing in all the major cities of the UK in the 1950s. But other young Irish girls also came to British hospitals for very different reasons. Can you tell me about meeting those young women and what their problems were?

I belonged to the Legion of Mary, and we used to meet young Irish girls down at Euston Station. When I joined the Legion first, I was working in Moorfields Eye Hospital. We'd meet the first train coming in in the morning, the mail-train. We'd watch those girls getting off the train at Euston. They hadn't got a clue where they were going, what they were doing. We'd go up and ask if there was anybody meeting them. There never was. I used to know if they were pregnant just by looking at them. Even at six weeks, I could tell by the shape of the nose. I had an eye for that. Helping those young pregnant girls became my mission in life.

'How far pregnant are you?' I'd ask.

Two months, three months was the usual reply. I could go back to my hospital and ring the Matron and tell her I'd got this girl who was a couple of months pregnant. I'd say we really needed more staff in the Nurses' Home.

'Right, Sister,' Matron would say. 'Give her a room.'

Matron was a Church of England woman, but she was a true Christian. She'd never turn any girl away, no matter what. We had so many girls there. I remember Annie O'Neill – she'd had a baby, but she had a drink problem as well. One night, when she was coming back to Queen's Square, Annie was in her cups and she went into the wrong room – and Matron was in the bed!

'Push over there, push over,' she kept saying. And of course, Matron woke up.

'What is wrong with you, Annie?' Matron asked her.

'Ah, Matron, it was Lester Piggott,' said Annie.

Matron was bewildered. 'Lester Piggott?' she said. 'What has Lester Piggott got to do with anything?'

'I won on the hosses,' said Annie.

Matron never even turned a hair.

We'd lots and lots of girls. I used to take them out to the Dames of Saint Joan out in Leigham Court Road. There was an Irish girl there that I'd met in Lourdes. She was wonderful. Whenever I met pregnant Irish girls who needed somewhere to stay, they would be taken into the home at Saint Joan's, a home for unmarried mothers, and they could have their babies there.

Saint Pelagius's was another home for unmarried mothers in Highgate, run by the Sisters of the Sacred Heart. It was a sister house to the one in Castlepollard. Anyway, these girls would have their babies and hand them up for adoption. But the rule for the Catholic Adoption Agency was that you couldn't adopt a baby once you were over forty-two. I thought that was daft – sure it's possible to have twins of your own at forty-eight! It did not make any sense to me – I used to have stand-up fights with Bishop Harvey over that ruling.

But bless Fr Francis – he was a wonderful man. He used to make it possible for so many Catholic couples who really wanted babies to adopt them. The babies would be born to the unmarried Irish girls who just couldn't keep them, so those births were never registered. The babies would simply be handed over very quietly to the adoptive parents, who would then register them as their own. Lord rest Fr Francis; he and I did what we believed was best. Maybe we'll have to account for it on the last day. Well, we did what we did.

There was a family once living in Edgware, a family with one child. The couple couldn't have any more children and they were absolutely devastated. 'Don't worry,' said Fr Francis. 'We'll get you a baby.' So we did. We got the baby, and he was registered to the couple in Edgware.

Years and years later, I remember this very lovely young doctor coming into Maida Vale hospital. I asked him who he was, and he said 'Doctor Keane.' I told him that we needed to know his first name, but he insisted on being called 'Doctor Keane'.

'I'm sorry,' I said, 'I'm not going to call you Doctor Keane – this is a family hospital, a friendly hospital, and you'll have to come around to our way of thinking.'

'All right,' he said, 'my Christian name is Patrick.'

'Really?' I said. 'And would your parents live in Edgware?'

'Yes,' he said. 'Do you know them?'

'I do,' I said, 'do they still have the newsagent's shop?'

He said they did.

'Well,' said I, 'the last time I saw you, you were only a baby. Now here you are, a doctor, all ready to tell me off.'

He said his Mum and Dad would be delighted to know that I was in Maida Vale Hospital, looking after him!

And that was the baby that Fr Francis and I had brought to the couple living in Edgware, all those years before.

Happy endings for some adoptive parents, then – but how did the girls feel having to give up their babies?

Some of them would be devastated. The last girl we had from Maida Vale, she gave her baby up, and I saw her some years afterwards. She'd gone back to live in Leitrim. She told me that not a day goes by without her wondering how the child is, thinking about him, about how he's getting on. But I can tell you, that child was far better off with his adoptive parents – they had the money to educate him and to give him all the important things in life.

I probably had about one hundred and fifty girls in that predicament over the thirty years I was at Maida Vale. And, of course, there were many other hospitals and many other nurses doing exactly the same thing.

There were women at home in Ireland who had their babies in homes like Kanturk in Castlepollard, but they were doomed. Until their child was adopted, there was no way of getting those women out of there. And, believe me, there were some nuns there and the softest part of them was their false teeth. I can remember one incident where three sisters became pregnant, and it was the same man who was the father of all three babies. Fr Francis went over to Castlepollard and he tried to get Pearl out – she was the first sister.

It was a terribly harsh place. The girls had to go out and milk the cows and work on the farm. They were slaves, absolute slaves. It was like the Magdalen Laundry, only on a farm. We got those three sisters out of there, one by one. I took them over to Manchester and they did their nursing training there. Nobody, absolutely nobody, knew anything about them at all, where they came from or anything else about their background. So they had a fresh start in life. Maggie, the youngest – she's my age – she's in Birmingham. She specialised in nursing the mentally handicapped.

But there were girls who had their babies and kept them – they stayed on here in England to live – and the grandparents back home in Ireland never knew that they had a grandchild. Those girls kept their secret. I admire the girls who didn't have a termination. I'd go to the ends of the earth to stop somebody having a termination.

There was a girl from Limerick once, though, and she really conned me. She didn't want anyone at home to know she had this baby, or so she led me to believe. I said that was OK. All my cash used to be spent on these girls – ferrying them back and forth, buying baby wool and so on. Well, I didn't smoke and I didn't drink, so that was my choice, to spend my money on other things. One day, I was crossing Camden Road and this man – Charlie was his name – called out to me 'Hi – Sheila! What are you goin' to do with that O'Donovan one?'

I didn't know who he was talking about. 'Who?' I said.

'The O'Donovan one – I saw you with her the other day, and I see that she's pregnant again.'

The girl hadn't given me her right name – and she was having her third little nipper! Anyway, she had the baby adopted – we were always very pleased when girls wanted their babies adopted: there were more people looking for babies than there were babies available. And now, with the pill, sure we have nobody at all!

There were thousands of young Irishwomen nursing here in the fifties. Why do you think nursing was such an attractive career for them?

There certainly were – in my hospital alone, in Manchester, when I came over first, there were eighteen girls from Crossmolina in

Mayo! You didn't have to pay, you see, your training was free. And I think that the regime here wasn't nearly as harsh as in Ireland.

I remember that a cousin of mine, Kathleen, trained in Dublin, in the Mater. As a young girl, I used to visit Kathleen whenever I went to Dublin – I'd go and spend the afternoon with her. There was a nun called Sister Mary over her, and that Sister Mary must have a good job shovelling coal in the next life. Kathleen fell foul of her once over a chipped teapot, and Sister Mary made her stand in the ward at visiting time holding a bowl of water. That was her punishment. I thought that sort of behaviour was out of the Ark altogether – and with a temper like mine, I probably would have murdered her. So that was one reason why I couldn't train in Ireland.

We had a very strict regime here, too, in terms of nursing training. But everybody was fair. We had Irish nursing sisters here, too, secular sisters, and they were all very fair.

Some Irish people have spoken of difficulties in getting accommodation in London. Was this your experience?

No, absolutely not. Never. While I was working at Moorfields, I lived with an old lady who had Alzheimer's. Her sister-in-law was a nurse and I knew her from the church. So we agreed that I would look after the old lady, stop her wandering, and in return, I got my accommodation very reasonably. I didn't need anything elaborate. Mind you, the old lady would come knocking on my door at half three in the morning.

'Are you there yet?' she'd ask.

'No, I'm not,' I'd say.

'Ah, well, you will be soon.'

Or else she'd knock and I'd say 'Yes, I'm here' and, God love her, she'd just answer 'Oh, well – goodnight, then.'

Then when I went to Maida Vale, I met a woman called Máire Graham, and she became my friend. She was a staff nurse, and she'd just had her baby. The flat where she and her husband Tom were living wouldn't let her stay because of the child. Lots of places wouldn't accept children. So they had to get out. But they hadn't got enough money to get a place of their own, so Máire brought her baby home to Wicklow, to her sister-in-law who had a child the same age. Máire had to leave the baby in Wicklow for a year, and she came back to work in Maida Vale. She and I became great friends.

I had a few pound saved and I said to both her and Tom 'For Christ's sake, take this money and buy yourselves a house.' So they bought their house in Kilburn and I moved in with them as part of the family. Tom had a place at home in Galway which he sold, so then we got a car. Then his mother moved in with all of us in Kilburn, eventually, to look after the little boy, Michael, while both Tom and Máire worked – and that was very common. Nanny used to look after us, too – she'd always have a good meal ready for the two eejits working in the hospital!

Tom died of bowel cancer some years back, but Máire and I still share the same house. She comes home with me on holidays to Ireland, too. You may think I was pure stupid – and maybe I was – but it all worked out very well between us.

I know that you are very active in your community, that you take part a lot in Church events. Was the Catholic Church always an important part of your life?

Yes. When you're working in a hospital, you come across people who don't practise the faith, who don't believe in anything. I get very worked up over things like that. But I had one wonderful experience with one of the doctors I worked with. His children, John and Cecilia, used to come into the hospital every Christmas to see myself and Máire – we always used to give them Christmas presents. Cecilia came into us one year with rosary beads around her neck and she said to me 'Sister, I'm going to be a nun when I grow up.'

Anyway, the following Christmas when she came in, she was

wearing a nurse's uniform – the child was about nine at that time. So she asked me if I liked her uniform and I said 'Oh, Cecilia, I thought you were going to be a nun!' 'I'd have to be baptised first,' was the response. Her father, who had gone beetroot red, then asked me if I knew anybody who might be willing to give his two children instruction so that they could be baptised. As it happened, there was an old nun in the ward next to us who had Parkinson's disease, and Cecilia's father was her consultant.

'Come with me,' I said to him, and we went to visit Sister Anna.

'Sister,' I said, 'how are you feeling?'

'Marvellous, Sheila,' she said to me, holding out her hand. There was no shake in it at all.

'Then how would you feel about giving two tiddlywinks instruction so that they can be baptised?'

She just looked at the children's father.

'Do you mean that?' she said.

He said he did, and that was that. The two children came every Saturday for instruction. The father had been originally Church of England, then he became a Buddhist – the man had been searching, searching for a long time – and finally he believed that the Catholic faith was right for him. I got great satisfaction out of that, out of his conversion. His wife had been a Catholic before she married him but, because they married in the Church of England, she had been excommunicated. So now she also took instruction and went to confession in Quex Road, and the whole family was received into the Church. It was wonderful. Things like that are very important to me.

You've lived around Kilburn and Cricklewood for most of your life. What sort of things did you observe about the Irish communities living there?

A lot of the young fellows who came over in the fifties were very lonely. They lived in one room, and it's no fun staring at four bare walls. So they'd go out for a drink, for a laugh, and some of them would drink too much. For others, they had too much money. They behaved badly – it's a lot to do with how you were brought up.

Some people felt a great sense of isolation. When I was in Manchester, to be Irish was to be part of the community. When I came to London – and I'm still in London, still living around the same area – there are people around the corner from me and I haven't a clue what their names are. They're not the friendly type. There wasn't the same sense of belonging.

And what about the Irish in Ireland?

I love going back to Ireland. I spend the month of June there every year. And I go back for Cup finals. I go to Lough Derg and to Knock. But I find things very changed. Houses seem to be springing up like mushrooms everywhere. I get very worried when I think of all those people owing so much money to the banks. It's a real concern, because I think the economic bubble is going to burst, sooner rather than later. I think we've lost the art of living within our means.

And there's a lot of suicides in Ireland, too. It's frightening. I think there's still a caring element in society, though – I wouldn't despair for Ireland, not at all.

Any regrets?

I wouldn't change my life. I suppose I've been foolish in many, many things, but no, I wouldn't want to alter anything. I was very fortunate, though. I didn't have to strain too much to get what I wanted. And I've always loved my work. I've always been very outgoing, too, so I've got to know everybody in my community, and we support each other. I know everybody; everybody knows me.

When I came to Maida Vale first, I used to take over the

Galtymore and run a dance as a fundraiser for the hospital. We'd get things that the National Health wouldn't support. And I still do things like that – run fundraisers for less fortunate people. I enjoy my life.

'In those days, you followed the work'

Tony Maher is a man in his mid-sixties, originally from Kildare and now living in Harlow. His forty-six years away from Monasterevin have not blunted his native accent one whit. He is a man of formidable energy and optimism.

You left Kildare in the mid-fifties and came to England. Did you come over in a spirit of adventure, or was it a case of economic necessity?

I left Kildare because there was nothing there for me to stay for – snagging turnips for three ha'pence a drill didn't appeal to me. I was eighteen when I left. Everyone was leaving at that time. The only people left behind were those who were joining the Irish Army. A lot of people were joining up then – that was when the war in the Congo was going on. A brother of mine joined up and he stayed on for twenty-one years: he did well. But then again, he didn't do a lot of soldiering: he was a blacksmith.

Funnily enough, I did go up to join the Army, myself and this other guy, on a deep winter's night. We were supposed to be signed in the next morning. They gave us a cup of tea and the corner of a crust, and then we were handed our bedding. So we went over to the billet and made up our beds.

But there was a dance that night in the Curragh that we decided we wanted to go to, only we'd no money. And the Guinness at that time was one and thruppence a pint. So Jim Carroll, the guy I was with, he had a watch and he sold it for thirty bob. Off we went, had a couple of pints – not too many – and went to the dance. We met two girls from Newbridge and we walked them home afterwards. The twelve o'clock bus was just about to pass, on its way from Dublin to Kildare, and Jim turns round and says to me 'Jimmy Dunney is playing in an all-night in the CYMS in Kildare – what about it, Tony?' So we jumped on the bus, went to the CYMS for the music and came out at three o'clock in the morning.

By that stage, it was a toss-up as to whether we'd go back to the Army base in the Curragh, or whether we'd just go home. We shuffled about a bit, and even the penny came down in favour of the Curragh. Ah, but I don't think our hearts were in it! We changed our minds and headed off home.

A few days after that, Jim left for England and I wasn't long following him. But I've often wondered how things would have turned out had I stayed and joined the Army. But other than soldiering, there was nothing at home to stay for, nothing at all. And you could come over to England for very little.

You went to Coventry initially. Why was that?

It just so happened that the people I came over with all were stopping in Coventry. There was plenty of work there, and I did well, earning two pounds or two pounds ten a shift. The first job I got was doing a bit of building work. There were a lot of Irish in Coventry in those days and I think I just accepted that – I don't think I found it strange to have so many Irish around me in England. An awful lot of them had come over years earlier – in the late forties, after the War. I think they probably got the brunt of the anti-Irish prejudice when it came to looking for accommodation.

But by the time I was there, things were different. There were so many Irish around Coventry that you were automatically steered in the right direction when it came to looking for digs. You'd go into an Irish pub, and someone would always let you know where you could go and be welcome. There was prejudice against the Irish, of course there was, but with so many of your own around you were able to avoid it.

Anyway, when you're that age, you don't dwell on anything for very long. You're thinking about the dance that you're going to, or what good picture is on. And your food was very important, because at eighteen you're always hungry. I remember when we'd come out of the picture-house in Coventry, we'd always go and buy faggots and peas. No matter how well fed you were in the digs, you'd still get a basin of this into you after the pictures.

I didn't stay long there, though – I moved on to Birmingham after about nine months and did shunting work on the railways. Everything was strange to me then – don't forget, I hadn't even been out of Kildare before I went to England. There were a lot of black people working on the railways in Birmingham, and I'd never seen a black person in my life before – not even one! Now I was surrounded by them, and I thought that they were strange-looking people. I found it hard to understand their accents, too, until I tuned into them.

In those days, you followed the work, so we all used to move from town to town. We'd usually get into the new town late at night and we wouldn't have anyplace to stay. So we'd go to the Salvation Army hostel – it cost a half-crown a night in those days – or you'd go to a Rowton House for the same money. Most of those places had fairly big rooms, with maybe six or eight beds to a room. You wouldn't know any of the people there, and, while nobody would do you any harm, they *would* steal from you! So the thing to do was, if you had anything worth stealing, you put it under the mattress. And you had to make sure your boots were safe. So you took them off, lifted up the legs of the bed and put one leg of the bed into each boot. When you went into the room at night, every bed had a pair of boots on its front legs! It was really funny to see, but at least they didn't get stolen.

Back then, even if you missed the last train, you could put your head down in the railway station and sleep for the night. You never even thought about anybody harming you in those days.

It was by and large a happy experience. But then, most places I went were happy experiences for me.

Do you think that had something to do with your own attitude?

Yes, I think so. I do indeed. You must remember, a lot of people of my generation didn't get a very good education. They'd listen to others giving out about the 'so-and-so English' – but they really wouldn't have formed a view of their own. It was ignorance, really: if they heard something nice about the English, they wouldn't think it worth repeating. It all depended on who they spent their time talking *to*. You'll always find that there are people who will tell you what they think you'd like to hear. In that sort of negative Irish company, very few people are going to stand up and say what a tolerant people the English are.

It didn't take me long to figure out the sort of company I was in and what sort of conversation we were likely to have. I heard so much about what a prejudiced people the English were, but I didn't just accept what I was told. I kept my eyes and ears open and I found that that view was wrong. And even more so now: I've got to know English people from all different levels of society and I've found them to be a most tolerant people. They showed great understanding, not just of the Irish, but of all nationalities who came here to make their home. I've found so many educated English people who would be more than inclined to take the part of an Irish person, or a person of any nationality, if they were in trouble – for example, they'll welcome the asylum seekers who are arriving in Britain today. They believe that there is plenty of room in their country for everybody, and they detest the type of people who pull the ladder up after them. Like, I'm sad to say, a lot of our people – they can be the worst in the world. Anyone would think that this was *their* country! Quite a lot of the Irish believe that asylum seekers shouldn't be coming here, to England, at all. Ask them why, and they don't know: they can't tell you *why*. They just know that they don't want them here, even though the Irish arrived in England in the same way. Some Irish people seem to forget that very quickly. Quite a lot of them are stirring up trouble for the newer immigrants. The attitude seems to be: 'We're all right now – the rest of you get out.'

I've always believed that you get treated in the way you deserve to be treated, no matter where you go – not just in this country. I think when the Irish arrived first, a lot of them tended to be wild and loud, and that frightened people. English people didn't understand that you'd just had a few drinks and were shouting and roaring, but that you didn't mean any harm. You might be making a lot of noise, but that didn't mean you were going to hurt anybody. But, to others, that sort of behaviour could appear to be threatening. Over the years, and it has taken time, the Irish have proved that they are as good as anybody else. And it's because of that – well, just look around you. The Irish are part of everything now. They're everywhere.

Were you aware at any stage of a shift in attitude towards the Irish?

Yes, I was. During the seventies, when things were bad in the North, there was a change in attitude. But none of it was ever directed at me, personally. By that time, we'd already been here a long time, and people knew us. It was hard to tell during those years who was the most embarrassed – the English people or the Irish. I took the decision not to pretend that the North of Ireland wasn't happening. I used to break down the wall of embarrassment by discussing the conflict with English people, by talking about it openly, and I found that that was by far the best way of handling it.

Everybody suddenly felt at ease, once the subject was out in the open. When you've known people for a long time and something like the North happens it's awkward for everybody – you have to find a way to talk about it.

There's a lot of ignorance here about Ireland – a lot of people here just didn't understand what was happening. But why should they? I mean, I'd go home on holiday to Ireland, to Kildare, even in the midst of the Troubles, and I'd hear nothing there either about what was going on in the North. I wouldn't hear a word about it until I got back here, to England. I used to think everybody at home in Ireland was aware of what was happening, and I'd say 'Isn't it shocking what's happening up North?' Well, I'd be told 'Shut up about the North. We don't want to know what's happening there.'

So how can you blame the English for not knowing?

Some of the finest people I ever worked for were English people. I remember one man I worked for asking me what in the name of God was going on in Ireland, why people were behaving as they were. I told him we'd have to go back a long way to explain. I said 'If you can tell me why someone would sit down in a room and starve themselves to death for a cause, if you can get inside the head of that man, then you will understand. Until you can do that, you'll never know.' But they *were* interested in knowing. The problem was they'd have to find the right people to ask, because they found it a very difficult topic.

You moved from Coventry to Birmingham, following the work. Where did you go to after that?

After nine months in Birmingham, I moved on to Bolton in Lancashire. There were a lot of building workers in Bolton, all following the jobs like myself. People moved around quite a lot at that time and so word would spread as to where the good jobs were.

In fact, I remember that word of mouth in those days would spread for just about everything. I remember word coming through that somebody's mother or father had died in Ireland, and they were trying to locate the man to send him home to Galway, or to Mayo, somewhere like that. There weren't any phones in the houses then, and a lot of the men couldn't write, so the word of mouth spread from one man to the next. We found the poor man in no time – the word had spread like wildfire. And the police were great at that time, too, absolutely great. People at home in Ireland would go to the police there with the news of a death and then the Irish police would contact the police here.

If somebody had to go home in a hurry, all the Irish working together would look after him, make sure he had enough money to do what he needed to do. We would always have a whip-around for whoever it was. There was no such thing as subdivisions among the Irish – in the building work, they were all very integrated. Each individual got treated as he should be treated. We'd get the fare together, and a bundle of money, and send the man on his way. There were so many Irish working together that it was easy. All of a sudden, someone would go around with the hat, gather up a good bit of money and send the man on his way home.

Did you go back and forwards to Ireland much during those early years?

No, funnily enough, I didn't. I've gone home a lot more often in latter years than I did at that time because, in my case anyway, time didn't mean anything. I wasn't aware of its passing. I was always moving on to *do* something, and time slipped by very quickly. When you're young, there's always something happening – there's girlfriends, there's dances, there's football matches, there's going to the pictures. And before you know it, the years have passed you by. I was the youngest of nine children, and, before long, three of my brothers were over here in England with me, and a sister. My mother and father used to come over here to see us. So, in a sense, I had my family on both sides of the water. There wasn't a great need to go home.

I always socialised with Irish people, too. That's what so many of us did, and that can be a problem. Now, I'm not saying that it's a mistake, but I'll tell you something: in some cases, it's as though some Irish people never left Ireland. They don't mix at all with English people. It's understandable, I suppose – but it means that horizons are never broadened that way. It's a bit like people who join the British Army here: they go all over the world, but they might as well never have left England.

They travel everywhere, but they bring their culture and their country with them.

What are your impressions of the Kildare you left behind?

Well, I got flung out of school at thirteen and a half. I got fed up of it. When I think about it, I didn't start until I was seven – because there was such a long way to travel – and I got thrown out at thirteen and a half. If you take out all I missed – all the times I should have been there but wasn't – from not wanting to go a long way in bare feet and cold weather, sure I hardly had any schooling at all. I know that, if you want to, you can always educate yourself. But still, there's not a day goes by that I don't regret the fact that I didn't get some sort of a proper education at the right time.

Back then, the school I went to in Monasterevin was all Christian Brothers. There were no lay teachers then – it was all nuns and Christian Brothers in our day. Now there's no Christian Brothers – it's all lay teachers. It's amazing the way things change. One of the lads I sat beside in school was the headmaster there until recently; he's retired now. Anyway, as I said, I'm the youngest of a big family, and it was my experience of school that everybody was categorised. All the Brothers and the priest knew who everybody was, so everybody was labelled, categorised right from the very beginning. As far as the teachers were concerned, I was one of those boys that was never going to amount to anything. I came from 'that family'. 'It doesn't really matter about him,' they used to say. But the pharmacist's son, who'd be sitting beside me, now *he* was important. *He* was going to go somewhere. And the sergeant's son: he'd amount to something in life. But not me: not from my family. There was a huge class-consciousness among the Christian Brothers.

What made it worse was that everything was that bit tougher if you didn't have a little bit of money behind you. You were going into a cold school every morning – there was no central heating in those days. If you didn't have the right clothing, and the right footwear, you'd freeze. And you were trying to survive the day on a couple of slices of bread and jam – very often, you'd have it eaten by the time you reached the school. You weren't thinking about your education – you were thinking about where the next meal was going to come from and how you were going to get warm. Where were your priorities likely to be in that situation?

When you look back at those times, do you ever feel bitter?

No. I don't. But that's because I am who I am.

About eight years ago, I was sitting down with a brother of mine who's four years older than me, and I started reminiscing about our youth and all the hoolies we'd had, all the lovely things that had happened in our home in Kildare. And he's sitting there looking at me with one eyebrow up and, after a few minutes, he says to me 'What the *hell* are you talking about?'

Eventually, I realised that he couldn't remember any of the good times that I was talking about – and I couldn't remember any of the bad times! But my brother couldn't forget them. He could only remember the rain, no sunshine at all. I was the complete opposite.

A little while after that I was going home on holidays, so I decided to ask around the rest of my family. Some of them were like me – they remembered all the wonderful times – and some of the others were like him, remembering all the terrible times. I certainly believe now that that is the way it is with people – it's got nothing at all to do with the times you lived in, or what happened you. It's something *within* people themselves, the things they choose to remember. Now, you might think that I was treated better by my parents than my brother was, but that's not the case. We were all treated exactly the same. I delved into this, because I needed to know what had happened. I don't know *why* it is, but I know for a fact now that attitudes like that have got nothing at all to do with how you were brought up, nothing at all. It's got to do with you as a person, whether you see the glass half-full or half-empty.

It's like when people ask me how I've found things over here: I've gone all through my life making the best of things.

One of the biggest helps in doing that has been my health. In my case, I always knew that I'd never need to go without. My good health meant that I was always able to go out and get a job. I could do work in the middle of winter that other people couldn't do, and get a few bob. I'd got great physical strength; other people used their brains, I used my strength. When I arrived in England first, there was plenty of work for everyone – it didn't seem to matter whether you had a skill or an education or not. The fellows with the bit of education maybe became pen-pushers, but there were jobs for everyone, if you were prepared to work.

I was labouring on a building-site, for instance, but I was able to get married and walk into Harlow and get a house.

What was it that brought you to Harlow in particular – via Coventry, Birmingham and Bolton – rather than anywhere else?

Well, I had two brothers working here in Harlow. And my mother – she was like an old mother hen – she insisted that she wanted to keep us all together, for safety. I was away from the others at the time, in Coventry – I was pretty secure and able to look after myself, but she wasn't to know that. She didn't like the idea of me being on my own. She wanted me to be closer to the others. Worrying is a mother's job and that's a fact.

I was lodging with this old lady, a Welshwoman. I used to get paid on a Friday and I'd go home after work, get dickied up and head off out for the weekend. I wouldn't get back home until Monday morning, or maybe sometimes Monday afternoon. I never went to work on a Monday because if you'd a jingle in your pocket at all you didn't bother with Monday.

My mother had kept on at my two brothers, Seán and Denis, to go and get me – and she'd take no excuses from them. So the two lads arrived on a Friday evening, on a motorbike and sidecar, after I'd left for the weekend. Mrs Loomis, my landlady, put them up so that they could wait until I got back. They knew that they daren't leave without me!

I rambled in late on the Monday morning, with a bit of a beard and a hangover, to be greeted by two irate brothers. I was stuck up on the back of this motorbike in my thin little weekend suit – no pullover, no nothing – and back we roared to Harlow. Anybody would think I was after committing murder!

So that's how I came to Harlow. I was just after celebrating my twenty-first birthday. I met my wife here in Harlow, too – she's half-Irish. Her mother was a schoolteacher; she was the best mother-in-law of all time. My wife used to stay at home looking after the kids, and myself and the mother-in-law would go off dancing. How about that!

A lot of Irish people's social activities revolved around the local Catholic church – was that your experience?

No, not around the church; that wouldn't have been my experience. Around things that were Irish, certainly. We had a Gaelic football team here in Harlow, and a hurling team. And then we used to have the card games, the 'twenty-five drives' and all that sort of thing. Harlow was fifty years old last year; I'm here about forty-six years.

For years and years I used to consider Ireland as my home – I suppose I still do. But the last few visits back home, I've seen such huge changes there that I'm not sure anymore. It's not that I don't like the changes. It's just that the way things have changed there means that Ireland no longer falls into my way of thinking about it. At one time, when I'd go back there on holidays with a few bob in my pocket, you'd meet a fellow with a flute or a fiddle and you could afford to buy him drink all day. You could settle yourself into the back of the pub and have a whale of a time, with several people playing and singing. You go home now, and there's a television sticking up in the corner of every pub.

Or on a Sunday, there'd be a crowd after first Mass with a few dogs, and you'd head off together through the fields to catch rabbits and hares for dinner. You'd go out hunting for your dinner! Somebody might have a gun and they'd shoot a few pheasant. Now you go home and people are going out to a restaurant for their Sunday dinner, paying fifteen or twenty pounds a head – now, how much of a difference is that!

People have changed there, too. I find now if I want to know anything about what's going on in my own village, the first thing I have to do is find somebody who's been over in this country, lived here, worked here and gone back home to Ireland. I can sit down with them and they'll tell me everything that's going on – all about the people, the work situation, and you can have a real, down-to-earth, heart-to-heart chat about it. Try to talk to somebody who has never left Ireland and ask them about the work opportunities or the wages and they'll go all round the houses. 'Ah, well,' they'll say, 'some jobs are better than others' – but they won't tell you what you want to know at all. They think that you want to steal their job, their house, their wife!

I never felt pressure to live up to other people's expectations of my success when I went home – but then, I've still got so many of my own family there that maybe it was different for me. At the same time, you'd never know what people were thinking, or what they were saying behind your back.

Mind you, I never cared either!

Do you have a dream of going back to Ireland, of retiring back to your home place?

No, no. I don't need to have it, in a sense. I've got so many family there that I can go home anytime I want, and I always have somewhere to go to. That's different to a lot of other people, I'd say. Sure my family fight over who's going to have me when I go home and I have to make sure to be diplomatic and visit everybody.

I have six children and only one of them – the youngest one of all of them – used to take a haversack, every chance he got, and go back to Ireland. We called him Brandon, and the first thing he did was go to Kerry to visit Mount Brandon. Now he's married to a Finnish girl and they're in Finland. But I know he's anxious to get back to Ireland. Then one of my daughters married a man from Cork and she lives in Fermoy.

But the others – well, when you're born here and go to school here, that's where the strongest ties are. And things are different now with work – there isn't as much leisure time as there used to be. When young people get married now, they automatically have a mortgage, and that cuts down the opportunities for travelling straight away. They're more tied than we were.

Has England been good to you?

Absolutely. I can't listen to people moaning about England, and I tell them off every chance I get. And I think that they don't really mean it. Maybe they give out so much because they think it's what others want to hear. If they were nailed down to tell the honest truth, I think they might feel the same as me. England has been good to us. And if someone asked me where I'd like to be buried – I couldn't give a damn. Never would have. When you're dead, you're dead, so that doesn't matter.

The only thing I'd have done differently is that I'd like to have got a proper education, if I could have. That's the only thing. I know it's never too late, and I think that overall, with what I had going for me, I've done well.

I'm happy with my life in England.

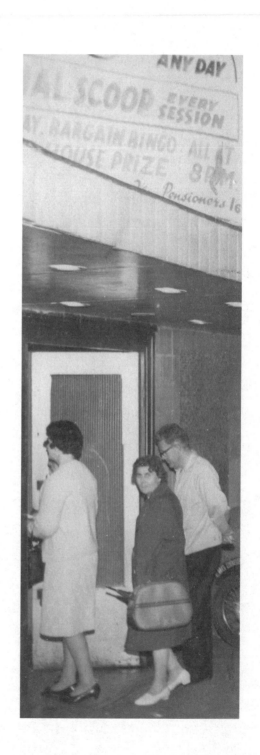

'STILL COLLECTING TICKETS FOR LONDON UNDERGROUND AFTER FORTY YEARS!'

Anne O'Neill is a gentle, soft-spoken woman in her early sixties. She has vivid memories of her childhood in rural Roscommon and of starting work in Dun Laoghaire at the age of twelve. She has spent nearly five decades in London and is currently looking forward to retiring after forty years with London Transport.

I understand that you spent part of your childhood with your grandparents, in a small town in Roscommon. What are your memories of those early days?

Both my parents were working in London, so I went to live with my grandparents in Ballymurray when I was a very young child, about two and a half. It was a terribly isolated place in those days. Not any more, of course – there are houses built up all around it. My grandmother was the postmistress there. We had no electric, no toilet, nothing like that. We had one paraffin lamp and I used to go down the hall and up to bed by the light of a candle. But it's funny, I never remember any house-fires back then; we all must have been very careful. We had to bring the water in from outside and we had a 'bath' using a basin. The toilet was wherever you could find a space – we were always looking to see who was missing out of the house. And you had to be very careful when you were picking up a dock leaf to wipe your bum in case you grabbed a nettle by mistake!

We had nothing in those days. I went to school in Ballymurray as a small child, and even then I had a little job on the way home. I used to have to gather enough sticks for the fire. Once I got home, I'd be sent off to collect two buckets of water. I suppose it was a round trip of about half a mile. I'd to go down the road, over the wall and across the fields to the well. I'd have to keep a good eye on the cattle, too – sometimes they could be very bad-tempered. I'd dip the buckets into the well – it was beautiful spring water, I remember – and then I'd have to walk all the way back. The size of me, carrying those buckets of water! I'd carry the full buckets a little way, then have to put them down to rest, then take them up again and so on, until I reached the cottage. One day, my cousin and I were sent to get the water together and we thought we'd be very clever: we brought the handle of the sweeping brush with us and hung three buckets on it. We got so far along, delighted with ourselves – and the handle broke in half! So we'd to start all over again.

I remember that we'd always pick mushrooms, too, after a shower of rain. We'd sit with a raincoat over our heads, waiting for the rain to stop. As soon as it did, there they were – but you could never see them until the rain stopped. Mushrooms would spring up everywhere, waiting for the picking. I went for blackberries one day, up to the gate lodge at Lord Crofton's. I remember I was wearing a little white dress. Well, suddenly, the heavens opened and I got a good soaking – my clothes were wet through. When I got home, my grandmother wouldn't believe me that I'd gone for blackberries – she thought I'd fallen into the stream because no rain had fallen around where we lived. Well, I can tell you I got a right hiding that night and was put to bed.

The following morning, she told me she was sorry. My uncle

had found out that I was telling the truth, that I hadn't been anywhere near the stream. But, God love her, she was terrified. 'What would I tell your mother if I lost you?' she kept saying. She was always afraid that something might happen me while I was under her care.

My grandmother kept hens and ducks and geese – we used to have to make sure to keep the half-door closed to keep them out of the cottage. She used to make bread, too, in the little three-legged pot that sat on the fire. And she often collected the water herself. There was a lot of hard physical labour in those days: it was a tough life. I remember my grandmother when her day's work was done. She'd just sit by the fire, looking into it, rocking her head up and down, up and down. But the day when we finally got a radio! Everybody in the vicinity came in to listen to it. It was a Sunday; we all listened to the football match. The kitchen was full of people: men in their caps, smoking their pipes, carrying their walking-sticks.

It was a real community event.

Your working life began in Dublin at a very early age. What are your memories of those days before you came to London?

My mother was working for a well-to-do family in London – her employer was an MP for Scunthorpe. She worked for him for quite a long time and he thought very highly of her. His name was Mallalieu.

They had three homes: one in Great Smith Street, one in Oxford and one in Carrickmines called Weetwood. Depending on where they were, so was my mother. If they were resident in London, she was there; if they were resident in Oxford, she was there; and if they came back to Carrickmines, that's where she was too.

I went to stay with my mother when I was about twelve or thirteen, in Weetwood, where she was working at the time. On Sunday mornings, she'd go off to Mass, dressed up in her coat and shoes, and I'd wait for her to come home. When she did, she'd take off the coat and shoes and I'd put them on. Then I was able to go off to Mass, properly dressed. When one of us was out, the other had to be in. That's the way it was.

Sometimes, I got clothes passed on from my mother's employers. They had two daughters and I used to get some of their coats and shoes. And there was a woman down the road, Mrs Parsons, and she brought up quite a lot of things one day, like underwear and blouses with buttons missing. I sat down and put buttons on them, or stitched them where they were ripped – maybe across the shoulders – and was quite happy with them. You didn't worry about things like that in those days. You took what came.

While my mother went to London to work, I was living with my Dad in Dublin. My father had had to come home from London at that time: he was unable to work because he suffered from scleroderma. His hands were all swollen up and he was in great pain.

He had worked in Scunthorpe for years, but himself and my mother had come home to get married and they stayed on for a while. He had to go back to England to look for work after I was born – the same hardship all over again. They were really unfortunate cases, those men – so many of them had to leave home to work, just so that they could put bread on the table. That was in the forties. Often what happened was that those men made new families in England and left behind what they had had here.

When he came back to Ireland in the fifties, he wasn't able to work any longer. There were very few jobs at home at that time anyway – things were terrible. If a woman got work, it was as a domestic and you were working from eight o'clock in the morning until ten, half ten at night. You got one half-day a week and the money was no good. Or else, there was restaurant work. I started work at twelve years of age, in the Miami Café in Dun Laoghaire, serving fish and chips. I remember working in a place in

O'Connell Street in Dublin, too – and it was not a nice place to be. My Dad was not one bit happy when he found out where I was working.

He was only fifty-two when he died. So then my mother brought me over to London. I was seventeen – that was in 1957.

What was your first job when you came to London?

I got a job as a domestic in a hospital in Wembley. I worked in the nurses' dining-room and that was all right. I took the job with a view to going nursing the following year. It was all a bit strange at first, because I'd just left home and everything was new and unfamiliar. In those days, we lived in, and that meant there was no longer the fear of losing the roof over your head. Any money you got was yours, because your keep was deducted from your wages before you got them.

When I went over first, I stayed for a few weeks with an uncle of mine who was a mechanic. I wanted to be a nurse, but this uncle felt very strongly that I should join the police force. I'd have had to go to college for that and my lack of education really held me back. I had no confidence as far as education was concerned. I got no more schooling after the age of twelve – in fact, I don't think I learned much after the age of eleven, because I was shifted from school to school. It was very difficult to keep up. I got rejected by the other kids which was very hard to cope with. I should have been at school until I was fourteen, at least. So the thought of going to college when I came over here to London was a pretty terrifying one. I couldn't have done it.

How did you survive your first few months in London, in what must have been very strange surroundings?

I used to go out quite a bit when I was here first. You could go down into London and have no fear. It was quite safe then – you could walk for miles and nobody would trouble you, really. I went out a lot with the other girls working in Wembley. We'd go to the picture-house and we used to go to the Galtymore, too, of course. In those days, there was no drink in the Galtymore. It was a huge community centre for the Irish – people would travel from all over to go to the dances there – my husband, Harry, used to travel up from Watford. I remember being there one night – I think we were dancing the Siege of Ennis – and this girl approached wearing the same dress as me. When that happened in those days, you tended not to wear that dress again. It didn't bother me so much, but the girl opposite me minded quite a lot!

In those times, for a dress or something like that, you'd have to save for three or four months – maybe more. My wages were three pounds one week, and three pounds twelve and six the next week, because we did what was called a split shift. It was very hard work – sometimes, all I was fit for was to go and lie down afterwards. I had one day off a week – either a Tuesday or a Thursday. We had breakfast every morning at half past five. There was a half-hour break later on, and I used to use that time to do my personal washing – hand washing all my clothes. We used to have to change our uniforms every day, too, at about eleven o'clock in the morning. Then it was back to the kitchen in time to serve in the nurses' dining-room. We were on our feet practically all day. We'd to do all the washing-up, all the serving, and you couldn't please the nurses making them tea. There was a theatre Sister there who was dreadful. You could never do anything right. No matter how you made the tea, it was never as it should be. There were a few women like that; they liked to throw their weight around.

I remember one of those Sisters on the day Pope Pius died. She came into the ward and looked at me and another Irish girl.

'Aren't you in mourning?' she said.

'For what?' I asked her.

'Your old Pope's died.'

We didn't get involved – she was just being nasty. We didn't want a row and there was nowhere you could go to complain about it, anyway. You might not be believed.

When we did go out to socialise, we weren't allowed to leave the hospital in our working clothes. Now you see nurses walking down the street in their uniforms, you see it here and at home. But in those days, we had to change out of our work clothes before we went out. I wasn't a nurse, but I came under the same strict rules. If you were caught walking the street in your uniform, you'd be sacked.

Once I started working in Wembley, I used to send my Mum ten shillings a week. She was back working in Ireland then, and she insisted I send her money each week so that she could save it for me. I used to put the ten bob in an envelope every time I got paid. All the Irish used to send money home back then. The postal orders used to keep so many families going.

My job in Wembley lasted a year, and then I worked in factories here and there. I worked in Smyth's Clocks and Watches in Cricklewood. It used to be a big employer, but it's not there anymore.

Many Irish people in London seemed to gravitate towards the Catholic Church. Did the Church play a large part in your life over here?

Yes and no. Sometimes I went to Mass, and other times I didn't. I never went looking to them for help either – I felt that there was really nowhere to turn to. I'd had an incident years back, at home in Ireland, that turned me off the Catholic Church a bit. My friend Marie and I went to the Pro-Cathedral in Dublin, and to go there you had to have money. This was in the fifties: you had to have a sixpenny bit before you could go to Mass in the Pro-Cathedral. Marie was working, so it was different for her: she had a bit of money. I used to watch herself and her sister go out at nights while I stayed in. I had to scrape the sixpence together – a thrupenny bit and three pennies. Marie went in front of me and put her sixpenny bit on the plate. I went to put my coins down and the man said to me 'No, you can't do that – it's got to be a sixpenny bit.'

Well, of course, I filled up with the humiliation of it. I went and stood outside. Marie was looking everywhere for me and couldn't understand where I'd got to. She and I are still friends, by the way – she lives down in Tottenham. Friends have always been very important to me.

I was quite young when that happened, and I didn't have a good response to it. It put me off religion. I looked out for myself after that.

Back in those days, too, someone would come around to the schools every so often asking if anybody wanted to be a priest or a nun. I had two cousins, sisters, and their Dad used to drink quite a bit. One day, somebody came to the school asking if anyone in the class wanted to be a nun. One of my cousins, the older one, put up her hand. The younger one, not wanting to be left out, put up her hand, too. Both of them went away to be nuns immediately. One was fourteen; the other was twelve. That would have been in the very early sixties. It was all wrong: they used to do that with the Christian Brothers, too – young kids who wouldn't have a clue what they wanted. Now, they got a good education, those girls. One of them became a teacher and then trained as a nurse. She eventually left after about eight years, but she'd got two professions while she was in there. The younger girl did stay and she took her final vows. You have to remember that the convent was an escape for them – it meant they were able to get away from their home environment, which was very unhappy due to their father's drinking.

Did you see much misery here among the Irish in London, due to alcoholism?

Really and truly, as I saw it in those days, people drank too much because they had nowhere to go. Nobody wanted the Irish or the blacks or people with children when it came to accommodation.

So one Irish person, perhaps, would manage to get a big house, and then they would let out rooms to others. But they'd have them five, six, seven to a room, with mattresses all over the floor. All around Kilburn and Cricklewood the Irish exploited their own. The consequences were that the blokes would have nowhere to go. They all worked on the buildings and what have you, so they used to come from work, go into the pub and get drunk. Then they'd go home to bed – and half the time their money would be nicked. And that was their life, because there was no life. If there was six of you on mattresses in one room, what sort of life was that to come home to? It was nothing. Those fellows did not have a drink problem when they arrived here – they developed it *because* they were here, living in conditions like that. It was a tough life on the buildings for the Irish.

The men used to be picked up for work outside the Crown bar in Cricklewood. But that's going to be gone, soon – they're turning it into a luxury hotel. So many of those men worked their whole lives and got nothing at the end of their years – no pension, nothing. Big building firms like Murphy's got rich on the back of men like that. They exploited their own. It happens with all nationalities – the blacks were exploited by their own people, too. The Irish and the blacks had a lot in common – they both suffered from discrimination. The Irish at least were allowed to go into pubs in those days – the blacks were not. They suffered a lot.

Harry had an experience once, when he went looking for a job. The boss was sitting there in this great big posh building and, once he found out Harry was Irish, he said he didn't want him, that he didn't want any Irish. Harry walked away, and then he turned back and said to him 'It was the Irish that built this place, and if it wasn't for them, you wouldn't be sitting there.'

The Irish were everywhere. There were a lot of Irish nurses in all the London hospitals, too – and there are still a lot of Irish voices there today. Kilburn, Cricklewood and Camden Town were alive with Irish. Kilburn is still a real village, although it's changing now. It used to be rough – too many drunks. They're putting in cameras and refurbishing a lot of places there. They're doing a lot of work like that.

Just like here – blocks of flats are being pulled down and replaced by something better.

I understand that many Irish girls came to London to have their babies in secret. What was it you observed about those girls and about the fate of their babies afterwards?

After my own little girl died, the Welfare Officer from London Transport came to see me. I think that's when the topic first came up. There were people like me, grieving over a dead child, and then there were others having children they didn't want – or *did* want but couldn't keep. London Transport was a pretty big concern in those days – they had everything, even a place where people could leave their kids while they worked. This Welfare Officer worked closely with the children that nobody wanted, or that nobody could take care of. London Transport looked after its employees very well.

Quite a lot of Irish women in those days had children fathered by black men. That, of course, was a complete no-no at home. If you went home with *any* baby in those days, you were finished, weren't you? So the women had their babies, paid money towards their keep and then they'd take them out for their birthdays and go and see them on their days off. I believe they were beautiful children. Some were eventually put up for adoption; some weren't. Some of the mothers just couldn't part with them, but they couldn't bring them home with them either. The women would go home to Ireland for Christmas as usual, leaving their children behind, and pretend that nothing had happened. Mind you, that didn't just happen with mixed-race children – many young women had babies here that their families back in Ireland knew nothing about. I've come across a lot of that.

And then there were those whose families *did* know – and who worked hard to cover the whole thing up. I remember a family that used to live close to me at home in Ireland. The daughter got pregnant by some young man who was engaged to another woman. So she came to London to have her baby and, of course, to avoid disgrace to her family. Her mother came over here later on and stayed for a while with her. Then they went home again together, and the mother kept telling everyone that her daughter hadn't liked London all that much, that she'd been very homesick and so she, the mother, had gone over to bring her back home.

That girl was never right after that. She was only eighteen. Her baby was adopted and the poor girl probably had no say in that – or anything. The important thing was that the disgrace had been covered up. There were many girls like that, even one within my own extended family. But it was always covered up. Those girls would be broken-hearted. There was a family I knew back home in Ireland. The mother died and the father was left with all the children – six or eight of them. All those children got into trouble – all the boys made local girls pregnant. One of those girls ended up in a home in Dublin; I remember going to see her.

Dear, oh dear. I was quite young at the time, but I've never forgotten it. There were four flights of stairs and she had to scrub every single step. She had to scrub all the way from the top to the bottom before she was allowed to see me. That was her punishment. She was eight months pregnant. It was very cruel. She eventually had that baby adopted.

When I had my second son, Gary, thirty-four years ago, I remember a nurse telling me about a girl she had looked after while she was nursing in Edgware. This girl had twins, but she couldn't give permission to have her babies adopted because she was so young. So her mother came over from Ireland to sign the forms and caused havoc, ranting and raving about the disgrace her daughter had brought on everyone's heads. This nurse took her aside and said to her 'You've got two beautiful grandsons. What do you care what the neighbours at home will say? What difference does it make? If you have these two boys adopted, don't think that it'll all go away. It won't. You will always be their grandmother – you can't give that away. Don't forget that.'

Afterwards, she said she was terrified she'd get the sack for being so outspoken. She was afraid that the grandmother would report her. But she didn't. The woman came back to her and said that she'd thought about what the nurse had said, and that she was right. Herself and the daughter went away with the two little boys, but nobody knows what happened after that.

It wasn't just the Irish, of course. Girls came from other countries as well – I knew Scottish and French girls in the same predicament. But there were quite a lot of Irish.

Do you think that you've worked very hard?

Yes. I think I have. I've worked full time all my life, even with five children. I've never worked part time. I'd never have been able to do it without the help of my family. My sister-in-law came to stay with us in the early sixties and she was a great help to us when the children were born. Then my mother joined us in the seventies. Between all of us, we kept the house and the kids going and both Harry and I have worked very hard all our lives. But it had to be done: it was a case of survival and getting a home together. I was married at nineteen, in 1959, and I've worked with London Transport all through my married life. I joined just after my Dad died, in June 1963. I've been there ever since.

It was very important to us to have our own home. I remember some of the places we lived in when were were married first, and they were difficult. We had one landlady, an Irishwoman, in a house in Cricklewood and we had to make an appointment to have a bath. The Irish were often tough on their own. You could only hang your clothes out on certain days, too – some of Harry's socks disappeared once. It wasn't funny: in those days you missed them. We couldn't afford to replace them.

We had to be in by a certain time at night, too, even though we were married. Doors were locked at eleven o'clock. We were never locked out, because we always stayed home. We had to get up for work very early in the mornings. But I remember that same landlady wanting to know on one occasion why we hadn't been to church.

It was often difficult to find accommodation. I can still remember the signs in shop windows 'No cats, no dogs, no children, no Irish, no blacks.' I regret that I never took pictures of those windows.

The first home we bought was where my first baby, Charlotte, died, and I couldn't live there anymore with the memories. She was born in 1965, on her Dad's birthday in July, and she died in December 1966. That house needed a lot of improvements anyway, and we were advised that we'd be better off selling, which we did, and we bought this one. We've stayed in the same area ever since, in West Hendon.

Working for London Transport was tough going. I worked shift – sometimes getting up at four in the morning for one shift, coming in at two a.m. after another. When I first started on the buses, on one route alone – the 113 – there were over a hundred shifts. You could never get used to the hours because they kept changing. There were difficult times, too, when there were bomb scares in London. They used to vacate the buses and the driver and myself would be left. Nine times out of ten, there'd be nothing. And there were lots of hoaxes. I remember a station being closed once because of a suspicious parcel. So we all waited until it was safe – and the policeman came out carrying a pound of sausages! That was the suspicious parcel.

In the very early days of the Troubles, a lot of Irish people were afraid to open their mouths. It was a very uncomfortable time to be Irish. Even where we lived, in Hendon, there was a bomb in the sorting office – twice. We could never figure out why. Why Hendon?

I'll never forget the day Staples Corner was bombed. My sister-in-law was sitting here, having a cup of tea, talking about something that had happened downtown somewhere. Suddenly, there was a great big bang – the cup and saucer started to shake with the impact. I was just about to push a plug into the socket, and I thought the bang had come from the electric. But it hadn't – it was Staples Corner being blown up. Quite a lot of the Irish were pulled in for questioning over that bomb.

But things were uncomfortable only in the early years – it got easier as time went on. Still, it definitely had an impact on your life – bomb scares everywhere put you off going out. We were never mixed up in anything like that, but we were always worried every time the kids went anywhere in case they'd be hurt. I was working over at Euston when all that trouble was at its height. My mother used to worry about me – things were always happening at Euston.

But I never found that being Irish went against me in my job – not at all. There were a lot of Irish working in London Transport – you couldn't get to know them all. Don't forget that the English wouldn't work on the buses or the Underground – they were always white collar. Working with London Transport was beneath them. I remember one day when I was getting abuse on the bus and this other passenger intervened. He said to the guy who was abusing me 'Oi, you – would you do this girl's job?'

'No,' says your man.

'Right then, leave her alone. If you're not prepared to do her job, and I'm not prepared to do her job, leave her alone. We're Englishmen,' he said, 'white-collar men.'

I think there's a change these days in the sort of jobs the Irish do. They've moved up and it's the eastern Europeans who are doing the building work. Now the Irish *own* the construction companies. I believe that even in Ireland itself the building workers are coming from abroad.

I'm working in Finchley Central Underground now – still collecting tickets after forty years!

How do your children see their own identity – are they Irish, English or happy to be both at the same time?

Both, I'd say. I've never heard them pass any heed on what they are. They mix well with everybody. We never took them back to Ireland. My mother was here from the time they were born, and Harry's from the North of Ireland and there was always trouble there – so we never took them back. The North's a very bitter place. Nobody here cares whether you're Catholic or Protestant – people just mix with each other and they don't pry into what you are or who you are. The downside of that these days is that you could be dead next door and nobody would know, or care. Back home is different; people are still more closely knit there, especially in the country.

I never went back once my mother came here to live with us. I'd nothing left to go home for. It must be twenty years since I've been back. I'd like to go sometime – my Dad is buried in Kildare – but I don't have any longing to go back and retire there or anything. My family is here. I know of people who have gone back and they're not very happy. A couple from Mayo that we used to know sold up and went back to Ireland. The wife settled fine – but he's back here now. Others have sold up everything here, gone back, bought a place – and it hasn't worked out. So they sell again and try to come back to London. But, because they're retired *and* just lost a lot of money in the move, they can't afford to come back to the places they used to live. So they lose out twice.

Then there was another man we knew, a carpet fitter from Burnt Oak. He couldn't wait to retire and get back to Ireland. Himself and his wife sold up and headed off, so looking forward to going back to live in Ireland. The poor man died seven weeks later.

We went to a retirement seminar recently. The advice was that you do not sell up and go *anywhere*. That goes for all nationalities – same advice for the Irish, the Jamaicans, everybody. Go to wherever you think you'd like to live and rent somewhere. Rent your own house out – don't sell it. Then wait and see.

I believe things have changed a lot in Ireland. A man I know from Cavan told me that the Irish are just building, building, building. He says that in the next four or five years there won't be any room left – the whole place will capsize! And people here say that the Irish don't have time for you anymore – you have to make an appointment to see anyone, including your own relations.

It's not like it used to be – we hear of stabbings, murders, theft. That's not what we remember, what we were used to. And there's everything around, drugs and guns and things.

It's just all very, very different from what we left behind.

You were saying that people came here in the fifties because there wasn't anything for them at home – they had to leave. Do you blame anybody for that?

I just accept it. I do think about it when I see the way people there are getting on today. It's sad that you were forced away from your home place, but you didn't have any choice. My Dad took ill and he only got seven and six a week. We had a little house in Cornelscourt, not far from the Magic Carpet pub. That cost ten shillings a week – that's why my mother had to go out and work. She told my grandmother that she'd have to put me in an orphanage because she just couldn't live. There were no benefits in those days, nothing. My grandmother wrote back and said 'No – I'll take her.' I was barely two and a half when I went to live with her.

It's funny what you think you remember. I was very young and, apparently, I took this fancy to a little chicken. I was always picking it up and cuddling it. Then one day, by mistake, I closed the half-door on the chicken and killed it. My grandmother told me that I picked it up and wouldn't let go of it. I kept going around saying

'Chickee dead, chickee dead.' I played havoc for three or four days with this chicken!

What does the word 'home' mean to you now?

This is home. My Mum's buried here, my daughter's buried here and my four children are around me. I couldn't just sell up and tell my sons to get out.

I'm happy with what we've been able to do for our family here. If I hadn't been working, we wouldn't have as much as we've got. Our children have had the best education we could give them.

So, yes, this is home. My 'heart home' and my 'made home'.

'WHAT AM I DOING HERE?'

Joe and Marie Dunne are a married couple in their mid-seventies. After thirty years in London, they returned to Ireland in 1976 – to Bluebell in Dublin, where Joe had been brought up. Marie had grown up close by, in Inchicore. They are intelligent and lively, and unafraid to express strong opinions about their experiences in both London and Dublin.

Joe, I understand that there was a particular event in your life, when you were twenty-one, that forced you to go looking for work in London. Can you tell me about that?

I was put into the railway, CIE, when I was fifteen. I had always wanted to be a carpenter, but for the first two years there I was a painter – painting wagons. And then I went to the sawmills to be a wood machinist. That was great because at last I was dealing with wood and learning all about the machines that made tables and everything else. But when I came twenty-one, that was it. They just let you go.

There were eight 'boys' – young men like myself – there at the time. We were all apprentice wood machinists. We hadn't got a chance: we were just the helpers. After they let us go, they took on another batch of fifteen-year-olds. We all knew we'd never get a job there – except for maybe one or two, if someone of sixty-five happened to retire. Otherwise there was nothing, no hope really. At that time it was accepted. Everybody went like that. You knew there was nothing, so you took the boat.

I went first, before Marie. My sister was already in London, and she brought me over. I think it was in June of '52 or '53, and I had a fiver. A fiver! I have a photograph somewhere of my first day in England. I'm lying in Hyde Park, asking myself 'What am I doing here?' Sunday afternoon, after travelling all Saturday night: a long old drive. A meal somewhere, and then lying in Hyde Park asking myself that question. 'What am I doing here?' I should be back in Bluebell, playing football.

What other memories do you have of those early days in London?

When I arrived, I got a job on a building site, digging ditches. The landlady wanted her money and you couldn't run to your mother for help. They were hard times. Money was bad, and you had to scrape and get any old job. Then you had to keep yourself as well. All you had was a room in a three-bedroomed house. I remember that a Mrs Staines was my landlady, number three Brixton Road, and I must certainly say she was a lovely lady.

But I never intended to stay.

I remember one of the happiest times of my life was coming home for Christmas that first year. I had to buy my ticket early in order to be sure of getting home. I'd also been paying emergency tax, and they told me I'd be getting a lump back. Getting that money, and getting the bus back from the building site, knowing that that night I'd be getting on the boat for home – that was a marvellous feeling. I probably had about twenty or thirty pound in my pocket and I felt wonderful. It was a fortune! But I'd no intention of going back to London, not really. I was home for maybe a month or six weeks that time, and I said that I didn't want to go back, I didn't like it.

But I had to. There was nothing for me here. The first job I got when I went back was in Bayswater, in the cinema. I was all togged up, dicky bow and all. I was on the door, chucking them out there in front of me. On my day off, I used to sit in the back of the cinema. I'd nothing else to do, nowhere else to go, like. I was in a room on my own, in some snobby place, somewhere in Bayswater, I think. So I'd spend my day off in the back of the cinema, watching some film I'd seen all the week before. I remember *one* of those films – *Shane*. That bloody thing was on for a week and it nearly drove me mad. Every time I see it coming on television now I say 'No, no! Please, no!'

Those days were an experience. I can't remember how long I stayed – a good long time, though.

Marie: My first trip to London was to visit my sister, just for a holiday. I couldn't get over it. I stayed for a while, maybe two months. I was about twenty-two or -three then. I knew that the sea divided Ireland and England, and I couldn't believe that they had roads and paths the same as us. It was all strange, really strange. I wouldn't say I liked it. And my sister used to encourage me to go home. I certainly wouldn't have stayed on my own, not if she hadn't been there. I probably just got to like London when Joe came back. He'd been in Dublin during the time I was with my sister – but he couldn't get a job, couldn't get back into the railway, so he'd no choice but to come back over to England. Anyway, we decided we'd get married in Ireland, and then we went straight back to London afterwards.

Did you know when you married that there was definitely nothing for you in Ireland?

Joe: That was generally known – so many people spent so much time hanging about. There was no regular work here in Dublin, nothing permanent. At least I had steady work in London. I stayed in Bayswater Cinema until I saw a job advertised in the paper for a wood machinist with the City of London. I went down for that and I got it. I used to have to get the Tube every morning. 'Mind the door! Mind the gap!' I liked it, though. It was a big place and we made all the butcher's blocks, big wooden tables, things like that. So at last, I was doing the thing I wanted to do.

I was happy being a wood machinist where I was in London, even though at that time there was very little money. I had to do a lot of overtime – a flat week's wages just wasn't on. We were living in Dunster Gardens, Kilburn. There were thousands of Irish in Kilburn in those days. I really don't know why – maybe because it's near to Euston Station, and you're on the line there. And on Quex Road there's a big church and a community hall. As a matter of fact, it was funny, I was in Quex Road at Mass one time – the Latin Mass, a beautiful Mass – and afterwards the priest was coming down the church, and who was it only a priest I knew from Bluebell. He used to visit my mother.

Did you have any difficulty finding accommodation when you lived in London?

Joe: No, none at all. We never experienced any prejudice against us when we looked for accommodation. My first landlady, Mrs Staines, was a lovely woman. Then when Marie and I got married, we lived in Kilburn in a house owned by a Jewish landlord, a terribly nice man. He was the only Jew I knew who used to give money away. He'd give my baby son a half-crown from time to time – a half-crown! The only trouble was, we couldn't afford to save it, to put it away in a gold box somewhere.

Marie: He was a lovely man. I'd meet him with the pram, and he'd take out this purse, a little tiny purse, and give me a half-crown for the baby, always a half-crown. I was glad of it. It really made a difference to us.

Joe: He always promised us the ground-floor flat, the garden flat. I used to do little bits and pieces of work for him.

Marie: I remember the people downstairs were Jewish, and the people upstairs also.

Joe: We were in the middle, and the people downstairs were moving somewhere, buying a house, and they wanted to sell us their keys. At that time, people sold their keys.

Marie: And they wanted three hundred pounds!

Joe: Three hundred! When wages were only seven pounds a week! The landlord, Mr Handelsman, went mad when he heard it. He said 'There's no-one selling my keys!' And he kept to his word; he kept his promise to us. When the people downstairs left, he gave us the ground-floor flat – with a *garden*! And a *cellar*! It was marvellous, wasn't it?

Marie: Oh, yes. He was wonderful to us. When the other people left, he didn't even lock the doors. He just called up to us that the flat was ours, and the doors were open. We had a sitting-room, a bedroom, a kitchen, our own toilet, a little room with a bath and the garden. A garden in London! It was really lovely.

Joe: Around the time that we got the ground-floor flat, I left the wood-machining place, because the money just wasn't good enough. I wanted something better. So I moved to Heinz, the food company. I did night work there, cleaning, and it was great money. I worked shift work, all nights, maybe six nights a week. As well as the good money, I was entitled to staff sales on the children's food, the baby food that Heinz produced. Our sons, John and Paul, lived on it.

Marie: He used to get the little tins for a penny, or tuppence.

Joe: I'd go down during my shift and get a note with what I wanted, and it would be left for me at the gate in a bag.

Marie: I remember the cooked apples and soups!

Joe: And we used to get beans for ourselves.

Marie: Beans and sausages!

Joe: I was there for about a year doing the cleaning, at nights, but it got a bit much. Paul was born then, and Marie didn't like spending so many nights on her own, so I applied to be put on to one of the electronic machines for sorting beans. I got that and I had to do a six-month course, learning about the machines.

These were the first machines in England with photoelectric cells. They used to scan all the beans and reject the bad ones. It was great! We worked in darkness, so as not to interfere with the lights on the machines. They were marvellous – they sorted twenty beans a second!

Of course, we had to set and reset the machines depending on where the beans came from – Hungary, Chile – we'd be told in advance. Some of the beans were too bright, so we'd have to bring up the lamps to take account of that, otherwise the photoelectric cell would reject all of them.

I've always been fascinated by electricity, and this technology was wonderful to watch. We had fifty-six of these machines, and we had to walk around them all the time during the shifts, looking after them. Six operators for fifty-six machines. The beans used to come in on a conveyor, and then there was an escalator up to the tanks, which were all automatic. The work went on seven days a week, even Sundays, but I always had two days a week off.

I got to know the girls who used to cook the sausages for the tinned beans, and they used to have them ready for my breakfast on Sundays. I'd go to the canteen and order an egg, and then I'd all the sausages to go with it. It was a wonderful place to work.

It was absolutely spotless, too. Every pipe was taken down at five o'clock every night – the pipes the soup used to go through – and all these stainless steel pipes would be cleaned thoroughly. The only glass we had on our machines was the iris, where the beans fell down. If we ever discovered a crack in the glass, the tank was closed off completely, and the contents were sent off at once as pig-food. We had to make sure to be spotless ourselves, washing our hands each time we touched the machine. They gave us three sets of overalls a week, a hat, a coat, and nobody was allowed into our area – no admittance!

They were powerful employers. Both my mother and father died during the time I was working in Heinz. Marie had to ring up to say I wouldn't be in. My father had died and I'd gone home for the funeral. Less than a week later, before I'd gone back into work, my mother died and I had to go back to Dublin again. And what happened then, Marie?

Marie: When I called, they were very sympathetic – they knew that Joe's father had died only six days beforehand. They asked me if I was all right. I was so independent, I said that I was and that the children were fine, too. They said they were coming out to see me, and I didn't know why. This lady arrived, and I could have got hundreds of pounds, if I had asked. I wasn't like that. I was too proud to ask, of course, and insisted that we were fine. She wanted to make sure I had money for the rent, for food, for this, that and the other. And that was the lady from Heinz.

Joe: And where else would you get it? As well as helping out with money if you needed it, they also looked after our welfare at work – they had a doctor and a nurse and a casualty place in the factory, on the site, where you could go if you didn't feel well. It was ideal. And every Christmas, Heinz gave a present to all the employees. All the men got one present, and all the women got a different one.

I stayed there for eight years.

Marie: The presents were beautiful – one year Joe got a Ronson table-lighter, and another time he got beautiful glasses.

Joe: The gifts used to come into the warehouse in September or October. They'd be stacked there, completely covered. Nobody would ever know what was in the packages, and everybody would be trying to guess. But it never got out until the day they were presented – it was always very well done.

Why did you leave Heinz, Joe?

I left because I wanted more. I was ambitious. There was a cardboard factory out in Southall, where some of my mates worked. That factory was due to move to a new town, to Harlow, out in Essex.

Dick Stack was a mate of mine, and he was the manager. A

Kerryman. Used to be a policeman in Dublin. Nicest man you could meet. He brought me in on his shift, made me learn the machines, and then I became an operator. I worked shift, making boxes. Then Dick left and went down to the new factory as foreman. I think he had a new house in about a week – because it was a new town, then. He got a beautiful, three-bedroomed house. Then it was my turn. He called me for an interview with the managing director, and I got the job in Harlow.

Marie: And you could choose your house – a two-bedroomed or a three-bedroomed house.

Joe: I was made a foreman, then, although I didn't know very much about it. I was still learning. I used to say to Dick 'What the bloody hell am I supposed to do with this?' And he'd say 'The other fellas don't know much about it either, so you can get away with it!'

Dick Stack had left the police here in Ireland because of corruption. He was a police driver, and he told me he could not stick it. He'd give tickets out around Blackrock, and the following morning the book had to go to the man upstairs. Dick's book would come back down with several pages gone – people using 'pull' to have their tickets cancelled. That was in the fifties, and it was happening all the time.

Marie: Dick was very straight, and he couldn't take the corruption.

Joe: Straightest people we ever met, Dick and his wife. We really loved them.

Anyway, I worked there in Harlow with Dick for three weeks, staying with my sister at weekends. And then I got a call from the Council – pick your house.

Marie: We couldn't believe it. A three-bedroomed house with a bathroom – all we had to do was put down our furniture. A beautiful house.

Joe: And a lovely town. So we stayed and stayed. We were there for twenty-nine years altogether.

Were you treated well generally, as an employee?

Unicases was a good company. The manager there was Indian, but the managing director was a real British snob. He'd walk through the factory each morning, his cuffs sharp as a razor. If he saw a cardboard box on the ground – and we made the bloody things – he'd stop and say 'If I threw a half-crown on the floor, would you leave it there?' I'd say 'No, Mr. Plunkett.' But the Indian fella was a genius. The Jesuits found him in Calcutta, reared him, educated him, and they found he had a photographic memory. He was an absolutely brilliant man. He used to invite us up to the canteen to play chess. All the jobs had five-digit numbers, and if you asked him the number of any job – say, Smedley's Beans – he'd be able to reel it off straight away.

He was fantastic. But he never went any higher. He stayed the manager. Because of his colour. That snobbishness was still there in jobs.

Do you feel that you suffered any prejudice in the workplace because you were Irish?

No, never. In Unicases, seventy to eighty per cent of the employees were Irish, and they were the ones to get promoted. They were good at their jobs – whatever they took up, they were good at it. After I was in Unicases for about six or seven years, we heard that redundancies were on the way. I took the few hundred pounds' redundancy and went back to the building sites in London, just for a few months. I worked as a painter. I remember wiping the rain off the windows before I started painting – if the clerk of works stood at the bottom of your ladder and couldn't see white paint, then you just didn't get paid. And it was a long run from Harlow to London – a good hour. I used to pick up a lot of fellas in an old van.

I worked on the lump – I needed the extra money. There was no security in it: you earned every penny you got. If you hadn't worked up enough hours by a Thursday, for example, they'd just pay you a quarter of what you were due. You had no cards or anything on the lump. Chances are, if you were paid for more than you'd done, you wouldn't come back again on a Monday. So they kept you short. Conditions were terrible.

And then, lo and behold, I got into the Council in Harlow, as a painter. I'd heard that they were looking for painters, to do all the council houses. In no time at all, I was assistant foreman. I'd take over when the foreman, a much older man, wasn't there. I used to drive the van around, managing all the other painters. There was never any resentment against me because I was Irish. In Unicases, there were a lot of English on the machines. They never resented that I, an Irishman, was their foreman. In the Council, it was the same. I was working with fellas and all of a sudden I was told I was temporary foreman. There was never any trouble between us – they just accepted it.

We all did well, we all got on well. You did, if you were prepared to work. I had some fellas from Dublin on sites, and they'd make a show of you, they would, really. Make you ashamed to be Irish. Rejects, they were. Not good enough to get a job anywhere.

We'd have sixty painters on a big contract – all nationalities. The West Indians were great painters. But these Dubs would make a show of you. They'd come in earlier than anyone else and nick all round them – they'd steal everybody else's paint supplies. We had to sack the whole site one time. It was mostly Dubs that caused all the trouble.

We brought almost everybody back after a few days, but not the Dubs. The English foreman, Bill, used to say to me 'My God, Joe, you're Irish, and look at these.' They used to threaten him and everything, and he was an old man. When you hear about English people treating the Irish badly, just think of these fellas. They'd get into a room in some poor woman's house and wreck it, through drink. That's all it was. Drink. They went out with nothing and they came back with nothing. You cannot afford to drink in

England. Every penny counts. During the week, we often had two pounds left to last us until Friday. And we made it last. You couldn't afford to be out of work.

And were you ever out of work due to circumstances beyond your control?

Yes, when I worked in Unicases, there was a strike. We were part of the newspapermen's union, Sogat. The printers went out on strike. I was the Shop Steward and the foreman, and we were all staying in. Then management came down from London and started bringing in scabs. The union told me there was no way I could stay in, not where there were scabs. So I had to come out, and the strike lasted a long time – something like fourteen weeks.

Don, the Indian manager, took me aside and said 'Remember this, Joe – you'll be the last man back.' He was right – he was my friend and he knew the union would let me down. They took the workers back in groups, ten today, twenty tomorrow. And I *was* the last one back. Don was teaching me a lesson – how I should never trust the union. He was teaching me to ally myself with the manager's side. He proved to me never to trust anyone else when it's your career that's at stake. I carried that lesson with me; I never trusted any union after that.

Anyway, while we were out on strike, the union offered us work in Fleet Street on the papers, cash in hand. They even put a bus on to bring us there and back. We'd go into the union offices and they'd tell us where to go – you go to *The Times*, you go to the *Mirror*, you go to the *People*.

We'd start at seven o'clock at night and do an hour on and an hour off. We'd walk around to all the other newspaper offices at three o'clock in the morning and one would give us a copy of the *People*, another would have a copy of *The Times* and we'd end up with copies of all the papers. Because by three all the papers were finished, on the chutes, ready to go. Then we'd hand in our number, collect our money, get back on the coach and go home again. We did that for sixteen weeks. Just on Saturday nights.

But I can honestly say I worked in Fleet Street!

How did you manage during those early days, Marie? Did you feel isolated, cut off from family and friends?

I didn't work outside the home after we got married. Beforehand, of course I did – I used to work in CIE, too, when I was single. I found it very hard, managing the home and the children and the money. I'd never had to do it before I got married, so it was all strange to me. I managed somehow, I suppose. By the early sixties, things were easier for us. The rent was three pounds a week, and Joe was earning twelve.

I had my sister close by, but she went out to work. But I'm very independent, and it didn't bother me being on my own. I didn't feel the need for friends or a social life outside my family. I don't know whether that's a good thing, but that's the way I was.

There were lots of Irish in Harlow, and I'd meet them when I went out shopping. We'd say hello and pass the time of day. But I was quite happy. My son John went to a Protestant school in Willesden, and when my mother heard that, she went straight down to the Oblates in Inchicore. The priest wrote to me – a very polite letter, saying that he remembered me as a young child. I ate my mother for that! I used to go and collect John at about three, and they'd all sing 'God Save the Queen'.

Your experience, both of you, of living and working in London and Harlow was a very positive one. So let me turn one of my questions around. Did you ever experience Irish people being negative about their host country?

Joe: Yes! I did. On building sites, and I'll tell you who was the worst: the Catholics from the North. I worked with all sorts of people. For example, there were a lot of Sikhs on the building sites in London – powerful men. They always worked on their hunkers. They built arches, brickwork – their work was beautiful. I used to wind them up, talking about 'this bloody Queen', and they'd say 'Me no understand you, me no understand you!' They'd be laughing away, and we all had fun, laughing at all the different cultures. But when the Northern Catholics were on a building site, there was trouble. It was terrible. They were always fighting – 'You English have part of our country', things like that. And the Dubs were the same. I never heard country people at it. But these buggers who couldn't even get a job in their own country – all giving out about the English. It happened a lot in pubs, too.

You must remember that ordinary English people knew nothing about Ireland. Absolutely nothing. I was working in Heinz when all the trouble started in the North in the sixties. One of the men who looked after the machines came to me and said he never knew that England ruled part of Ireland. I said 'You do – you're in the North.' But he never knew. Politicians knew, but the ordinary people didn't bother.

I detest those who give out about the English. They're usually the sort who has never been out of Dublin. Take me – my sons are English. And a million more like me – their sons are English. Paul and John class themselves as English, and I would never change it. I remember when Paul was small, playing with a neighbour's child, and, in fun, I tapped him lightly on the back with my shovel and I said 'Now, that makes you an Irishman.' And little Tom from next door, I had to tap him with the shovel, too – he wanted to be an Irishman as well!

All our second-generation children – they're all English. So when you criticise the English, you are criticising our own.

Marie: I remember we were getting ready to come home once, and I was talking to my neighbour, who was English. She asked me 'What are you going back there for, with all that trouble?' I told her there was no trouble where we were from, but she couldn't accept that. She didn't know anything about it.

Joe: It's only really lately that English people know about Ireland, through holidays.

We should forget about 1916, forget about all that happened – look at Germany today. Six million Jews massacred, and we're shaking hands with Germany now, after only sixty years. Yet we go back hundreds of years to blame the English for what happened in Ireland.

Did you find any change in attitudes towards you when the Troubles were at their height?

Joe: Only on one occasion. I was working for a contractor and he used to go to the armaments in London to paint, underneath the ground. And I wasn't allowed. No Irish were allowed. That was because of the Troubles. But it wasn't just the Irish. They wouldn't allow anybody who had a prison record to work there either.

Marie: And that was for security.

Joe: Yes, because the whole armaments store was held underground. So, naturally, when the Troubles were on ... and I didn't take offence at that. I understood it. Even when we were coming home on holiday during that time, we were getting searched and watched going into Holyhead and that. We did feel it. And that underground job was a great one – a long contract and very good money. But there were no Irish allowed.

Marie: It was understandable, wasn't it?

Joe: Of course it was.

When you moved from Kilburn to Harlow, you were moving from one Irish community to the other. Can you tell me what Harlow was like in the fifties?

Joe: Harlow was an old town, an old village that got built up, really, wasn't it?

Marie: Yes, but everything in it was brand new. There were lots of Irish there, but it was also very mixed. There were more English than Irish in the cul-de-sac we lived in. We never had any trouble, never had any words with anyone. And I'm just remembering our landlady in Kilburn. When we were moving, she even gave us the name of a removal man who'd do a good, competitive job for us. I remember when we arrived in Harlow, the van met us, and the driver had to ask us where our house was. Nobody knew where anything was, it was all so new.

Joe: It was a marvellous place. The town was brand new, but there was countryside all around us. We went down country lanes on our way to London. We had the best of both worlds.

Marie: When we arrived at the house that first time, there was a bag of coke, a pint of milk and a loaf of bread. The Council left that for the people who were moving in new.

Joe: You wouldn't get it anywhere.

You both had family members within reasonable striking distance, didn't you?

Marie: My sister Rita lived in Kilburn, but she often came to stay in Harlow.

Joe: And I had a sister in Harlow. People always had somebody. Everybody brought someone else to the town. That's how they moved in and made new friends.

Was the Catholic Church an important part of your lives?

Marie: We always went to Mass. Perhaps if we'd needed help, we'd have asked for it. But we didn't need anything. We were content.

Joe: There were lots of churches in Harlow. Gilbey – the gin company – owned all the land in Harlow, as far as I know. The Council bought the land off Gilbey to build the houses – and we're talking about hundreds of houses, you know. I heard that Gilbey insisted on sites for the Catholic church, and the schools, and they're all situated at corners in the different districts.

Marie: Where we were, there was no church, and they used to have the Mass in the school hall. The caretaker went on holidays, sometimes, and the hall was locked. So Mrs Gilbey used to invite everyone up to her house to celebrate Mass. We didn't have a car at the time, and once she drove me and John and Paul back home. When she drove into the cul-de-sac, she said 'Now you know where I live, you must come and visit me.' Of course, we didn't, but she was a lovely lady.

There were clubs attached to most of the Catholic churches, but we didn't mix much – we didn't go to the Irish clubs or the pubs or anything like that. When you don't drink, you don't mix that much.

Joe: That's very true. When you go to any of those halls, it's a lovely social night, but everybody has a drink, and we didn't do that.

Marie: But I never missed that – I didn't *want* to do it.

You've said that England was very good to you. What made both of you decide to come home?

Marie: I'm sure that Joe will say differently, but my sister, Rita, and her husband, Benny, came home, and that left me with nobody. I kept saying to Joe after that 'I think we should go home. I think we should go home.' And Rita bought a cottage in Oldcastle, Co. Meath, and she kept telling us how great it was. We decided that Joe would come home and see if he could get a job here.

He came home for six months and he had a job in Killeen paper mills. I wanted to live in Rathcoole, if you wouldn't mind, but that wasn't possible. Joe didn't want to live in an estate, because when he lived in Bluebell it was country. He found a house in Kildare with an acre of land and painted a lovely picture of it. He came back to Harlow and that was it. We packed up and headed for Kildare.

My God. When we got there, we couldn't even open the gate.

It was a jungle. My brother-in-law Paddy told us to get back on the boat! It was dreadful. An outside toilet. Stone floor. It was in a dreadful state.

Joe: When we came back at first, I'd had enough of being in England. I'd never intended to stay. I'd always wanted to come back to Bluebell, to this place here. But I've been very disillusioned. If I had my time again, I'd have stayed in England. What I see going on around me saddens me. Things are so different from when I was a young man.

What sort of changes have you seen?

I see the most corrupt people in the world, I think. I was working with English on building sites all my life and they wouldn't steal *that*. An Irishman will nick anything. Some of these English people did not believe in God, but they would never steal anything on you. An Irishman would take a paintbrush on you and never leave it back. They were always at that. I used to keep a pound in my glasses case, keep it in the office when I was the foreman, like. Someone got in and stole the pound out of my glasses case – I'd no money going home that night.

People here nick in the shops all the time. And what's really worse is Irish people buying something that fell off the back of a lorry. I'm not a 'holy joe', but I do believe that those things are not mine to take. I hate this 'I got that cheap, do you want one?' I do not want one!

I saw people at Mass, lay people, giving out communion. Giving out the sacrament on a Sunday and the day before with timbers stuffed up under their coats, stealing. An Irishman will take anything and think nothing about it.

Seeing teenagers today distresses me. We were starving in our house as teenagers. I was hungry every day. We had nothing because there were sixteen of us. But we didn't dare misbehave. And young people here behave badly and get away with it. And those who won't work! I've far more respect for the asylum seekers, and they're not allowed to work. That's not fair.

When I went to England, it was different. People had scruples, or morals or whatever you'd like to call it. Not here, not anymore. And look at the courts – people do wrong here, judges or whatever, and they give them a pension! Burke and Charlie Haughey – they still have their pension.

I don't know what has happened in this country. The country is still beautiful, but the people have gone down and down and down. They'll lie and steal and cheat.

I lived all my life among people who made no claim to believe in God. For thirty years, I lived with people like that, and I like them better.

And the people here think that they are saints.

What sort of expectations did you come home with? How did you hope things would be?

Joe: As we left them.

Marie: That's right – we expected to find things as we'd left them.

Joe: When I came back first on my own, it was January, I remember. We weren't allowed paint on the sites because of frost. I had a little Mini van, and I just packed it up and drove to Holyhead. Took me blinkin' hours on the M5. I came over here and stayed with Marie's mother. And then I bought a house in Kildare. I didn't know what to do about work. I had nothing – but after paying a thousand pound deposit on the house, I wasn't going to lose it. But I stood and looked at the house and said to myself: 'What am I after doing?' No money, no job, no nothing.

My brother was in Killeen, the paper mills, so I got a job there too. I used to travel in from Kildare to Clondalkin to work – it'll just show you. Nobody else would do it. But I had the Mini, so it didn't cost me much in petrol. Then a fella told me there were painting contractors needed in the Curragh. So I thought 'That'll do me!'

Then I saw these fellas in white overalls from the Board of Works, and I went to the Commandant to see if there were any vacancies. There weren't, but he encouraged me to call again. I did. Every fortnight for a year. Then in August, he told me I had a job. And the Kildare people, all they wanted to find out was who did I *know* – politicians, or priests or what have you. I said I knew nobody, that I'd got the job on my merit, no 'pull' involved. They were all amazed. I ended up wallpapering all the officers' houses. Some painters only like working with the brush, but I'll do anything. I earned their respect that way.

I loved working in the Curragh. I made great mates.

Marie: I couldn't believe the attitudes when we came back. Now, our neighbour in Kildare was a very nice woman, but she would do nothing to help you. I remember asking if she knew anywhere I could get manure for the garden, and she just said 'Oh, any farmer.' And then I found out that her brother was a farmer. What happened was, the house that Joe bought had been for sale for a very long time, and she had hoped to get it for next to nothing.

Joe: They'd wanted to buy the house and knock the two into one for themselves. But that didn't work out for them. So when I drove up in my Mini, that was the end of that.

Marie: I think that the Irish are dirty now – there's a big change since we went away. I think I expected things to be the same – you think your mother and father are there and all your family are there. I also think Ireland has become an alcoholic society. All the young people we see are drinking. One neighbour had to throw out her fifteen-year-old son because he was drinking. And he must have got into a row in the pub, because they all came around to the house and smashed in her windows. I think it's tragic.

Joe: The great word with young people today is 'partying'. They've no interest in politics, only in having a good time. Once they've money in their pocket, off they go, partying. And then they come to work on Mondays, sick as a dog. Watching young people drinking makes me ill. Fifteen- and sixteen-year-olds here getting served in the pubs, drinking and carousing – we hear them on their way home afterwards. When you think of what it can do to you, to the kidneys and liver of young people. It's bad enough for older people.

And yet there's all this fuss about tobacco. I know tobacco is bad – everyone knows tobacco is bad. But drink is worse. Even scientists are saying that. Smoking really only affects the smoker, but drink affects the whole household. How many houses are there where everything got banged up and kids went wrong over their fathers' and mothers' drinking? Last time the government put fifty pence on cigarettes and nothing on drink. And the politicians won't condemn drink because they drink themselves.

Marie: My sister Kathleen and I would meet in a pub for a sit-down and a cup of coffee. Young girls would come in with their babies, and, when the babies would cry, the dummies would be dipped in the Guinness and given to the baby. We saw that time and time again. And the reason we went to the pub was that the café across the road wouldn't sell you a cup of tea unless you bought a cake – and not only that, if you asked for cream in your coffee, they charged you extra for it. All we wanted was a sit-down and a chat. So we used to go over to the pub. But in the pubs, all the young people were drinking pints. Or – and this is something I can't stand – they'd be drinking beer out of a bottle. Even women on the buses drink beer out of bottles.

We see them standing outside the pub at half ten on a Saturday morning. We go shopping in Thomas Street and get all our fruit from the dealers. And not only do we see them waiting to get into the pub, but, from the night before, there's nothing but vomit everywhere, all over the road. And it's not only the men.

I wouldn't go out at night. I'd be too worried. It never used to bother me, never concerned me at all. But here, one day last May, something happened me. It was a beautiful day, and I was going into town to buy curtain material, around lunchtime. It all happened very quickly – my bag was pulled out of my hand, and the man jumped into a car. I just stood there, like a fool. I had a jumper that I was bringing back to Marks and Spencer, a jumper I'd never worn. I don't know whether it was the colour, or what.

My glasses, my travel pass, a hundred euro and a few photographs. A motorist had seen what happened, and he gave us the number of the car, a Northern registration. We reported it, but we never heard anything, and we won't hear anything. And now I'm afraid to go out. When I went to bed that night, I locked all the inside doors, and I've been doing that for months. After it happened, I couldn't even make it home, I was shaking that much. When I got to the door, I just slid down onto the ground. People don't realise what a thing like that does to your nerves.

Joe: And what makes me mad is that nobody does anything about it. You have Ahern who thinks more about Europe than he does about us. Nice Treaty this, Nice Treaty that. With that Treaty passed, this country will be a ghost country in six years' time. All the big technology firms will go to Poland and places like that. I worked with Poles – they're brainy people, and very hard-working. There'll be no jobs for young people here now that the Nice Treaty is passed.

At least I had someplace to go in the fifties. Young people today have no place to go. England is gone; America is gone.

What about changes for the good? Have you noticed any of those since you moved back to Ireland?

Joe: The greatest thing here, as I'm always telling my sister, is how they look after pensioners. It is the best in the world.

Marie: I agree with that.

Joe: Anything you want – you just go to them with a genuine case, and you'll get help. We have a doctor, free television, help with the phone bill, free bus pass to go anywhere you like. In England, you just get a free bus pass for your district; you can't go free from one district to another. We often go to Cork for the day. And the health service is much better here, too. It's gone so that you have to wait for everything in England. And when you do get your time, it's all a rush. But not here. Marie got the best of treatment in the Eye and Ear. I was in Naas, after I fell through a scaffold. I got the best of treatment in the hospital.

Marie: He was in for the week before Christmas and I was at home in Kildare on my own. I was so lonely. And I couldn't drive! The parish priest brought Joe home on Christmas Eve, and I had nothing at all in the house. Nothing in – at three o'clock in the afternoon of Christmas Eve!

I really never felt at home in Kildare. The house was beautiful, bigger than our house in Bluebell now. But the minute we turned down that lane, the first time I saw the house, I really thought that we were leaving civilisation. There were only six houses in the lane, and I was always very lonely.

I've felt much more at home once we moved to Bluebell. I love it here. You've only got to walk across the road to get the bus into town, and yet you're out of the city as well. I'm very happy to be back.

Joe says he'd like to go back to England, but I wouldn't.

Joe: We must be about twenty-five years home now. The only thing that's keeping me here is that this country is good to pensioners. Apart from that, it wouldn't cost me a thought to go back to England. Since we've come home, I've often asked myself 'What am I doing here?'

My mother's dead, most of my brothers are dead – that's it. I always said that one day I would do it, that I would come back to Ireland, thinking that I would have what I had once left. But I was disillusioned. Disillusioned with the people, not the country.

When you think of Sinn Féin getting seats here. Mass

murderers, the horrors that they did. I know that the Unionists were just as bad, but we're talking about Irish people here. Look at Gerry Adams, shaking hands with Irish children. He's a murderer. And the working-class people are adoring Sinn Féin councillors, and they don't know what's behind them. It is very sad.

But if I was to go out and criticise Sinn Féin at that corner there, I'd have a visit with stones through my window. And they talk about a democratic country. It's sad for such a nice country to have such horrible people, people who do not think right about what they are doing. I don't like Ahern – but even if he's taking brown paper envelopes he's better than Sinn Féin. Those people are murderers.

Did you, and any of the Irish people you were friends with, blame anybody for the fact that you had to emigrate in the fifties?

Joe: I blame de Valera. My mother was a de Valera woman, but I blame him for everything. He had a vision of what Ireland should be – his vision, only *his* vision. One man shouldn't have a vision like that for all the people. First of all, he wouldn't give three lousy ports to the British. And he did that in the name of Irish people. Look what we were fighting – there was never anyone else as bad as Hitler in the world. And yet, de Valera said no, we won't give you the ports.

He built up the hatred in everybody against the British. And he made a show of me and every other Irishman when he signed the book of condolences for Hitler. He was the only head of state to do so. What a blemish. And he never even said 'sorry' when it did come out about what Hitler had done. Even the first newsreels about the concentration camps, people thought that they were British propaganda.

And another thing, I went to Inchicore School here, and I was starving. I used to go down the canal to school, no shoes on my feet. I couldn't speak English in the yard. I was made, forced, to speak Irish. Had I been a Galway man, I wouldn't have been able to speak English at all. I had to emigrate: if I'd listened to de Valera and my teachers – all from the West of Ireland, by the way – I wouldn't have been able to speak a word when I went away.

My father had been in the British Army, and even my mother, the de Valera woman, said that the best food she'd ever got was from the Army barracks. They used to bake bread there and open up at ten o'clock every morning for the women. They'd sell the loaves for a penny each.

Even she had to hand it to them for that.

Marie: My father was an IRA man, and all he got was a medal. All these houses here in Bluebell, these were all British services houses. And all the ex-servicemen got a pension. It was only seven pounds a week, something like that, but it was worth having.

I met an old lady in Kildare who told me that every April, the British Legion would give her a lorry-load of turf, and when her husband came out of the army – now I'm going back – they gave her a donkey and cart for to go around and sell the vegetables. She would really praise the British Legion.

Joe: They were marvellous. There were people who died here, and for what? But I would never join an army for any country. I used to see the British soldiers coming back home after the Second World War, and I had a better job than them. I told them that myself. They'd spent years fighting for their country, and I used to meet them in factories afterwards. And what did the British government think of them? Nothing. Even the women, who'd endured six years of bombing in London: the government thought nothing of them once the war was over. And look at America – there was no place for their soldiers either, once the fighting was over. There's no way Bush will be out there fighting. People should remember that. I'd fight for no country. I'd fight for this house, but not for a country.

De Valera could have done a lot more for Ireland. He was the only man ever to escape from the British. And how did he escape? He was an informer. They let him out: nobody ever escaped. Who killed Michael Collins? Who sent him to England and tried to blacken his name? And my mother used to claim that de Valera was a hero.

He's no hero.

Do you think that modern Ireland has produced any heroes?

Joe: Seán Lemass, now, he was a great man. That was the man that started it all here. That was the man that brought me home. He did everything right. If we'd have had a few more like him afterwards, it would have been better. He brought in industrialisation and opened the country up to everybody, I think. I often read about what he was doing here, and I never believed it.

Things were booming here in the late seventies: there was work for everyone, but you still had the sods on the labour. It is wrong. It is wrong for you to be out working while other people live off your tax. I have much more respect for asylum seekers. They are like what the Irish were in the forties and fifties. We see them on the bus, spotless.

Ireland is becoming more multicultural. Do you think we have anything to learn from the UK experience?

Joe: I saw a lot of changes in England before we left. I didn't agree with the Labour party bringing in thousands of people. Look at the ghettos in Southall and Ealing – Indian ghettos. English people told me that they had to get out of those places. And the same thing is happening here.

You can't just bring people in and leave them – you have to supervise them. And don't give them permits for life – give them permits for five years. And then after ten years they can have a regular passport. But they hand them out here good-oh to anybody who has the money. And that is wrong.

Looking back now, do you think that making your own way in London at a young age meant you had to grow up very quickly?

Joe: Yes, I do. I feel terrible because I wasted my young life in England. I missed out on friends and parents, on playing football in the street, on just being a young man. I used to play football for Bluebell when I was twenty-one. When I went away to London, all that finished for me, but the rest of them carried on. I felt hard done by – cheated out of a young life with friends and family.

In England, we were always dashing around, looking for work, keeping going – and then you look around and you're forty. And it wasn't just me. I've seen people in England, particularly people from the West of Ireland, young Connemara men on building sites digging footings, with no skills whatever. They used to huddle together, speaking in Irish. It was pathetic. Other people used to laugh at them; they were like people from another planet. They'd never left Connemara in their lives, and here they were, on building sites in London, while the fat cats here were getting fatter. That was wrong. Give them the Irish language, by all means, but give them something else to go with. Particularly at that time in the fifties, because you *had* to emigrate. They, and me, and people like us, went over on cattle boats to England.

I used to see those poor lads from the West of Ireland and they could keep nothing. They'd go to some of the Irish centres, to a dance, and they'd take one drink. Then another, then another. They drank through loneliness. There should have been something else for them, apart from the bar. I don't know why every centre had to have a bar. It just encouraged lonely people to drink and spend their money. And so they'd come over with nothing, and they'd go back with nothing.

You had to keep everything going every day. There was no chance to take things easy. I hadn't even got time for Paul and John, my own children. I had to go out and do work in the evening time. That's where I lost out. I did some painting to earn extra money. Paul was always beside me in those days; I couldn't go anywhere. He'd always ask me where I was going and I'd say: 'I'm going to see a man about a dog.' And it would have been lovely to have had another couple of years with my mates in Bluebell – once I moved away, I never saw them.

But if I had stayed in Ireland, my career would have been very different. I had no forward drive to me. But in England, I had to have it. It was dog eat dog over there, for jobs and different things. If I'd stayed in the railway, I wouldn't have had to think. I'd have got my money there, year after year, home at a quarter-past five every night, every weekend off. Monday to Friday, every day from eight to a quarter-past five, for forty or fifty years. Mind you, there was great security, a good pension, but it would have done me no good.

In England you had to go for it. I often had to leave jobs because I knew they wouldn't last. I was always thinking about the next step, the next job. Even now, you can never say 'I'm well settled'. If anything happened to me, Marie wouldn't be able to cope with this house on her own, so it wouldn't cost me a thought to go into an apartment. You have to keep up with the house – you don't want to let it deteriorate. In many ways, I think a two-bedroomed apartment would be lovely. The time will come when I've had enough of the garden.

I'm seventy-five now. Your mind changes after seventy; never make plans before seventy.

Marie: Joe thinks of tomorrow; I think of today. I take life as it comes. I never felt any sense of bitterness about going to England. I was the youngest, and all the others were working, so we were OK. We used to go on holidays every year. We had a little house on the line in Greystones – CIE owned it, but my father rented it for a half-crown a week. There was nothing in it, only beds – no furniture. We'd go down there for long weekends, and I just took all that for granted. That's the way we were, and you can't help how you were brought up. I know that Joe's life was very different – I didn't have that kind of hardship.

Do you think that emigration brought its own hardships, despite the success you've both enjoyed?

Joe: I remember coming home for Christmas when John and Paul were small. We were in a boat called the *Princess Maud*. Christmas time, the weather was always rough. We'd a six-hour journey from Euston to Holyhead, and then, at three o'clock in the morning, we'd to get out into the freeze at Holyhead. There was a gale blowing. We had to stay up on deck with Paul, a little baby, being sick. But we had something to look forward to! The best bit was the journey on the steam train from Dun Laoghaire, seeing all the houses on the way into the city. That was great excitement. We'd only twenty pound, but it didn't matter.

What *did* matter was that we had to face going back to England afterwards. And that was pathetic. You'd see all the children crying as their fathers got back on the train again, going out to Dun Laoghaire. That was the saddest time, watching the children waving to their fathers and crying. I used to see old men going back on their own, not able to come home again until the next Christmas. They just didn't have the money.

I saw it on building sites all my life. I used to send my mother home a pound a week, and she was glad of it. I'd see the other people on a Monday morning, coming off building sites – that's when they used to do it. Country people, putting a pound into a registered envelope to send it home. You couldn't send it in an ordinary envelope – so it was costing you even more money. You'd want to see the amount of money that came into this bloody country from people like that.

Then people here have the cheek to speak badly about the English. That is wrong. English people are just like us. We're all only a few minutes away from each other by plane.

Why should we allow some politicians to keep the wheel going, to feed the hate?

Galtymore Cricklewood

SUN TONIGHT **24th OCT**

RAY LYNHAM

AND THE

HILLBILLIES

THURS SPECIAL SPOT **28th OCT**

TOMMY SEE

& THE CAJUN SOUND

SATURDAY SPECIAL SHOW **30th OCT**

EVER POPULAR

JACK RUANE

SHOWBAND FROM THE WEST

AND THE

GALLOWGLASS

CEILI FOLK BAND

SUN RIP ROARING **31st OCT**

RED HURLEY

AND THE

NEVADA

SHOWBAND SENSATION

Please do not throw this handbill on the road or footpath

Printed by Connaught Lithoservices Ltd. Tel: 01-731 0900

GALTYMORE — CRICKLEWOOD

SUN TONIGHT **13th FEB**

NEW STYLE   OLD FAVOURITE

DERMOT   **O'BRIEN**

AND THE   **CLUBMEN**

FOUR BAND FEAST

SUN " THE DADDY OF THEM ALL ! " **20th FEB**

BIG TOM AND THE **MAINLINERS**

Please do not throw this handbill on the road or footpath

Printed by Connaught Lithoservices Ltd. Tel: 01-731 0900

Postscript

'HOME IS ALWAYS SOMEWHERE ELSE BECAUSE
IN EFFECT IT CEASES TO EXIST'

'The past and memory, the immigrants' curse.
Especially the Irish. The Irish pushed out of Ireland
were left with one thing and that was their memory,
their own hidden Ireland. Of course they handed it
on to their children. What else did they have?'

Joe Horgan, *The Irish Post*

THE 'PLASTIC PADDY'

Identity. Belonging. Home.

In one guise or another, these three issues kept coming up for
discussion, time and again, among the Irish living in London.
What makes a home? As an Irish immigrant of some fifty years'
standing, do you now belong in Ireland or England? How do you
decide? Are your children Irish, even though they were born in
London boroughs, attended London schools and speak with a
London accent? How do they respond to the loaded term 'Plastic
Paddy'?

Or what happens when you or your children 'come home' – for
good? Is the reality for all immigrants that of 'essentially ... not
belonging anywhere'?[1]

Phyllis Izzard thinks that it is. 'I must admit', she says, 'that there is a sense of me not belonging in either place ... I very often have the feeling of being neither one thing nor the other.' Identity for second-generation Irish men and women can be a highly charged issue, perhaps because of their consciousness of their parent or parents' emotional attachment to Ireland. We can assume that children of the 1950s' emigrants attained adulthood sometime in the 1980s. If their numbers suggest that they had to be a very significant ethnic minority at that time, research published in 1985 suggests otherwise:

> There has been a conspicuous lack of attention
> directed towards the children of Irish immigrants in
> Britain. Perhaps it is because of their numbers, their
> familiarity, and their phenotypic similarity to the
> indigenous population that the second-generation are
> not usually expected to be experiencing the problems
> faced by the children of non-white immigrants.[2]

It is startling to find that second-generation Irish men and women also seem to have been 'invisible' in ways similar to the generation which preceded them. Their very 'familiarity' and 'similarity' were precisely what conspired against making them, and their particular needs, visible. The whole question of identity, however, did indeed emerge as a major issue in the lives of the young people surveyed: 'It was clearly not the case that they [the second-generation Irish] had been assimilated to a greater extent than the other minorities, or that they had escaped the many problems traditionally associated with second-generation youth.'[3]

However, just as there is no one typical emigrant experience, there seems to be no typical second-generation coming-to-terms with identity either. Kathleen Morrissey says that her own six children reflect two realities: one son and daughter are 'very much for Ireland' and four daughters are 'quite happy to be half-Irish and half-English'. Tony Maher feels that of his six children two have a great affinity with Ireland, while the other four have their 'strongest ties in England'. Phyllis Izzard feels that her sons were always 'quite content to be English' although they loved Ireland dearly, while Anne O'Neill believes that her family manages both nationalities 'hand in hand'. However, Joe Dunne is emphatic that his sons 'are English', and uses this to support his argument that when Irish people criticise the English 'we are criticising our own'.

'THERE'S AN AWFUL LOT OF BEGRUDGERY IN IRELAND'[4]

So what happens when 'our own' decide to return 'home'? What sort of welcome is there for our returning emigrants, those first- or second-generation Irish who decide to take their chances in twenty-first century, post-Celtic-Tiger Ireland? Not surprisingly, there is no simple answer to this. There is, however, a distinct wariness among Irish emigrants towards the whole topic.

On the one hand, there is the difference between what people feel is their 'heart home' and their 'made home' – a very useful distinction articulated first by Phyllis Izzard. All of the London Irish I spoke to were content that they had made their home in their adopted city to the best of their ability. Most realised that the time for 'going home' had passed them by – even if Ireland was where their true home, their 'heart home', lay. They were too settled, too tied by bonds of children and grandchildren, too afraid to make a move which might result in nothing but trauma. It is interesting that their apprehension centred mostly around how they would be received in Ireland, rather than any difficulties inherent in leaving their London home behind.

Fr Fullam recounts the experience of some of his parishioners in 'going home'. 'There can be resentment [in Ireland] of other people who do better, particularly with regard to material riches. They [the returning emigrants] are greeted with "You're only a blow-in!"'

Joe Horgan is a second-generation Irishman who made the move to Ireland from England four years ago and comments on the transition in regular articles for *The Irish Post*. He reflects somewhat ruefully that, although he knows Ireland well and has spent a lot of time here over the years, 'I'm an outsider here and in many, many ways I always will be.'

Kevin Casey agrees that returning emigrants can be regarded as outsiders, remembering that, even in the Ennis of his childhood, those who had been away were inevitably marked out as different. One who had been to America was regarded as 'no longer an Ennis man'. Instead, he was 'Old Doyle, the Yank'. Kevin recognises a certain begrudgery in Ireland towards the returning emigrant but remarks that 'they never said "No" to the money that was going back all over the years, even long before the fifties'.

When in one year alone, 1961, the Emigrants' Remittances (£13.5 million) virtually equalled the costs to the Irish State of primary and secondary education *together* (£14 million), his point about begrudgery seems well made. [5]

'WE EXPECTED TO FIND THINGS AS WE'D LEFT THEM'[6]

'The past and memory,' writes Joe Horgan, 'the immigrants' curse.' Memories of how things used to be surfaced amid a good deal of emotion when those who had been away for fifty years stopped to consider the Ireland of today. All agreed that the biggest problem for the returning emigrant was expecting to find the Ireland they'd once left behind. They either know this personally, because they've made that mistake themselves, or anecdotally, having seen too many of their peers fall victim to that particularly cruel illusion.

In Anne O'Neill's experience, couples who sell everything they've built up in London to follow their dream often have to face a bitter reality: one spouse settles, perhaps, the other does not. Others try to make the transition work, but it doesn't. And others still 'sell again and try to come back to London. But because they're retired *and* just lost a lot of money … they can't afford to come back to the places they used to live. So they lose out twice.'

In one way or another, all the interviewees believe that Ireland has changed radically, and not all for the better. Obvious things such as the availability of jobs, improvements in housing and the fact that people no longer have to leave their home place because of economic deprivation are celebrated. But the divisive nature of affluence, the increase in violence on the streets and the rates of suicide among young men are all causes for grave concern among the emigrants. The fact that 'all the old ways have changed', according to Tony Maher, leaves people less sure that today's Ireland is somewhere they'd like to come back to – even in the event that they could afford financially to do so.

People are aware of stories, too, of those who waited and hoped for fifty years to go home, living almost their whole lives in the future tense. The only thing to look forward to was the day they turned towards home. Many a homecoming was abruptly shattered by the unexpected death of one spouse or the other, leaving the bereaved to live out the remainder of their lives without the network of friends and family they had left behind in London.

In Joe and Marie Dunne's experience, the move home over twenty-five years ago was a mixed blessing. They, and Mary Walker, have great praise for the way in which pensioners are treated in Ireland, declaring the system 'the best in the world'. But, for Joe in particular, coming home in the belief that 'I would have what I had once left' was a disappointment. Corruption, an alcoholic society, the vulgarity that goes with sudden and excess affluence – that's what Joe and Marie see around them in the Ireland of today.

Joe now sometimes asks himself the same question he asked on his arrival in London, fifty years ago, as he lay on the grass in Hyde Park with a fiver in his pocket: 'What am I doing here?'

'MANY YOUNG MEN OF TWENTY ...'[7]

To have the resources to choose where you live and how you live is one thing. To be forced to accept anything you can get, due to ill health or bad fortune, is quite another. For those London Irish left on the margins of society, there is often little choice. Recent years have seen a noticeable increase in organisations dedicated to helping elderly Irish to repatriate, should they so wish, or at least to re-establish contact with family, often after many years.

Some of this work is done by the Aisling Project, 'managed by the London Irish Centre and Novas Ouvertures – one of the largest providers of services to the homeless in London' and elsewhere.[8] Trips are organised for the homeless Irish migrants 'who have lost contact with friends and family in Ireland, and who now have little social life outside their own community in the hostel'.[9]

According to Catherine Morris, many of these individuals, suffering from alcohol-related and mental-health problems, had been 'too embarrassed to go home' at any earlier date. They had lost contact with family and felt 'too ashamed to return to a prosperous Ireland' which they felt would not welcome them. The Aisling project encourages family reunions, but many of those who travel to Ireland after decades away refuse to contact family. They still suffer from that legacy of shame which accompanies their lack of success in Britain. Their return to Ireland is enough: they feel 'overjoyed' to be back – if only for a week's holiday.

The St Brendan's Village Project at Mulranny, Co. Mayo, run by Dr Jerry Cowley, provides sheltered accommodation for those elderly Irish who wish to return home and have some small resources to do so. Such accommodation enables them to leave difficult or unsuitable conditions in Britain behind. It includes both 'high support' and 'low support' housing units, all purpose-built to cater for the needs of its residents.

It seems that problems with physical and mental health are 'part of the package' for all migrants and 'the Irish migrants who have taken the short route "across the water" are no exception to the global pattern', according to Michael J. Curran.[10] However, it is startling to learn that 'Irish immigrants had the poorest record of physical and mental health of any minority in Britain,' according to the *British Journal of Psychiatry* in 1998.[11] They are fifty per cent more likely to commit suicide and are the only migrant grouping 'whose life expectancy worsens on emigration to Britain'.[12]

Undoubtedly, these figures conceal many complex and interrelated problems, some perhaps caused by the emigrants' own lack of coping skills, others by the society which may have treated some of them with hostility. One factor in all of this may also be what Fr Jerry Kivlehan of the London Irish Centre calls the 'conspiracy of denial' in Ireland about the fact of emigration. He claims that for years the Irish government refused to acknowledge the reality of emigration – even to the extent of 'deleting it from correspondence'.[13]

He recalls making strenuous representations to the Department of Education in the 1970s to include a module on emigration for secondary school students. The reality, he says, is that there has always been 'significant emigration from the West of Ireland, and yet nothing in the Irish education system recognised this fact'. It was simply unacknowledged, unconsidered. And so, young people continued to 'take the boat' with no more preparation than the generations which preceded them.

Such lack of official consideration for Irish emigrants was highlighted by the welcome visit of the former President, Mary Robinson, to the London Irish Centre at Camden. 'The initial Irish government response to her visit was a negative one,' says Fr Kivlehan. He sees this negativity as symbolic of successive Irish governments' unwillingness to 'acknowledge the contribution' of its emigrants. Mary Robinson, on the other hand, did much to highlight the practical and emotional resonances of the Irish Diaspora. After decades of denial, there was finally a tangible, visible recognition of the fact of emigration. Fr Kivlehan continues:

> Ireland hasn't even begun the debate about emigration. In the same family, you can have two

> brothers – one forced to emigrate, the other forced to
> stay at home. Both end their lives feeling bitter, both
> feeling they got the bad end of the stick.

The totality of both of those experiences needs to be discussed, debated – and accepted by Irish society. Father Kivlehan feels that such a wide-ranging debate is long overdue. We need to come to terms with the conditions which a whole generation of Irish men and women had to endure in the 1950s – both the conditions that forced them to leave and those that prevented their return.

Seeing attitudes towards the Irish change in 1980s Britain 'from hostility to acceptance', does not absolve us from the necessity of understanding the experience of an earlier generation. Many of the problems of the marginalised Irish, stemming from the 1950s exodus from Ireland, still need to be resolved.

EMIGRANT LIAISON COMMITTEES

Kevin Bourke, former Chairman of the Irish Emigrant Liaison Committee, Mayo Branch, remembers the first time he became aware of the impact of emigration on his native county. As a young boy, his Saturday job was to cycle around his local area, delivering money orders to the isolated farms where people 'were waiting at the door for me to arrive'. Mayo has been ravaged by emigration since the Famine, arguably more than any other county in Ireland. The value of the 'emigrant remittances' is very much acknowledged here.

It is not surprising that the Emigrant Liaison Committees originated in Mayo, although Kevin Bourke stresses that the Committee was founded to help all Irish emigrants, not just those emanating from Mayo. Working closely with agencies such as the Simon Community and local-council-funded Irish Centres in Britain, the MELC funds initiatives to help the less fortunate, the marginalised Irish who still live in Luton, Coventry, Birmingham – all over urban centres in the United Kingdom. A recent grant of €25,000 from the Department of Social, Community and Family Affairs will enable the Committee to 'host a seminar for returned emigrants to give them practical advice and information about making the move home after many years abroad'.[14] Among other issues, the current Chairman, Tom McAndrew, hopes to explore the potential for 'great disillusionment' when elderly emigrants return to their home place, expecting to find what they once left behind.

However, Kevin Bourke is not impressed with the government's record in holding out a helping hand to emigrants, returning or otherwise. For example, the Díon Committee of Ireland, which provides funds for the homeless and socially isolated abroad, and supports the excellent work of agencies such as Simon, had its funding cut by five per cent recently. Kevin Bourke feels that last year's report of the Task Force on Policy Regarding Emigrants has already, in effect, been shelved. Such a response is indicative of the lip service paid by official Ireland to its emigrants, of an attitude of denial which goes back longer than fifty years.

'I COULDN'T … STOP REMEMBERING'[15]

On St Patrick's Day, 1943, Eamon de Valera made his famous speech about 'cosy homesteads' and 'frugal comforts'. Now, sixty years later, we need to look again at the 1950s, at the Ireland that forced an entire generation to leave home, repeating the experience of a previous half-million who had departed in the 1890s, while they in turn followed the trail laid down by the survivors of the Famine.

That many prospered and succeeded in other places is not the issue here. What matters is that they were denied the opportunity to do so at home; that no matter how 'successful' they became, the grief and loss which inevitably accompanied such displacement were immense.

In Timothy O'Grady and Steve Pyke's haunting novel *I Could*

Read the Sky, a nameless Irish immigrant lists to himself all the things he is capable of doing. It is an act of defiant self-definition, a way of carving out a psychic space for himself in a hostile and utterly foreign city. He reassures himself that he is still vital, alive and worthy of dignified acknowledgement: 'I could mend nets. Thatch a roof. Build stairs. Make a basket from reeds. Splint the leg of a cow. Cut turf. Build a wall.'[16]

What he could not do, however, even after many years of London life, was to 'Remember the routes of buses. Wear a collar in comfort ... Acknowledge the Queen ... Follow cricket ... Understand their jokes ... Kill a Sunday. Stop remembering.'[17]

'Emigration', says Fintan O'Toole, 'has been the single biggest fact in the seventy-five year history of the Irish State.'[18]

Isn't it time we addressed it?

NOTES

Chapter title: Joe Horgan, 'Irish i', *The Irish Post*

[1] Joe Horgan, 'Irish i', *The Irish Post*

[2] M. J. Curran, *Across the Water: the acculturation and health of Irish people in London*, Edmund Rice Resource Centre, 2003, referring to P. Ullah, 'Second-generation Irish youth: identity and ethnicity', *New Community*, 12 (no 2), 1985, pp. 310–320

[3] P. Ullah, 'Second-generation Irish youth: identity and ethnicity', *New Community*, 12 (no 2), 1985, pp. 310–320

[4] See Kevin Casey's interview

[5] *The Irish Times*, August 2nd 1999

[6] See Marie Dunne, Joe and Marie Dunne's interview

[7] Title of drama by J. B. Keane

[8] *The Irish Post*, January 25, 2003

[9] Ibid.

[10] M. J. Curran, *Across the Water: the acculturation and health of Irish people in London*, Edmund Rice Resource Centre, 2003, p. 19

[11] Ibid., p. 11

[12] Ibid., p. 35

[13] Interview with Fr Kivlehan, 2nd May 2003

[14] *Irish Independent*, 7th May 2003

[15] Timothy O'Grady and Steve Pike, *I Could Read the Sky*, The Harvill Press, 1997, p. 35

[16] Ibid.

[17] Ibid., p. 71

[18] Fintan O'Toole, *The Lie of the Land: irish identities*, New Island, 1998

Acknowledgements

Thank you again to all of my interviewees, for their time, their candour and the warmth of their welcome.

Sincere thanks to the Shirley Stewart Literary Agency in London for its limitless support and hospitality. Also to Annie and Peter Howell of Harlow for their generous welcome and for introducing me to the Irish community there.

Thanks, too, to Mary Hennessy and Patrick Hennessy of Burnt Oak, and to Des Kelleher, Evelyn Kelly, Charlie Ruane and Margaret Walshe of Harlow, for agreeing to share their reminiscences with me.

I am indebted to Catherine Morris for helping me to understand the plight of the marginalised Irish in London, to Bill Moore of the London Simon Community and to Fr Jerry Kivlehan, who continues the very necessary work of the London Irish Centre at Camden.

Thanks to all at the Galtymore Dance Club in Cricklewood, both for providing a venue for interviews and for lending photographs from their collection.

The assistance provided by Kevin Bourke of the Emigrant Liaison Committee, Mayo Branch, and Deirdre and Michael Mullen of Castlebar was invaluable – thank you all.

I am also grateful to all at New Island, in particular my editor Emma Dunne, for their support throughout the ups and downs which inevitably accompany an undertaking like this.

And finally – thanks to Anthony Glavin for his faith, enthusiasm and dogged determination to see this done.